THE COMPLETE WINDOWS 10 BOOK FOR BEGINNERS

BY

Dr. ALFONSO J. KINGLOW

PREFACE

After reviewing many different books on Windows 10 and not finding basic information that would explain to a beginner or senior the structure of the software, what it did and contain, the hidden tools and resources, and how it function within the different versions, I decided to write this book with new information and some that I included in my other books, explaining the individual parts and how the user could benefit from this knowledge; and the new technologies that became available. I wanted to put it all in one place, so that beginners and seniors could find the information in one place that would help them understand how to troubleshoot and use all of the hidden tools in Windows 10 OS, that is not available in other books, to manage and setup their own computers.

Technology is advancing so fast, that at the first publication of this book, many new Windows Software and Standards with new advanced technologies that became available, and I include in this book to provide the users with the latest technology and standards that will impact Windows, so the users may benefit from these technologies.

The Diagnostic Tools are explained and where to find them as well as the built-in Windows System Tools. I show how to use The MMC or Microsoft Management Console and how to create "Snap-Ins" to Manage and troubleshoot the User Computer. These tools are built into Windows, but are hidden from the users. I talk about SECPOL and GPEDIT and others, that enable the User to Setup and Manage his or her own Security on their Computer.

This book would then contain information from all of my other books that would be in one place, and new recent information, where the user would find all what they were looking for explained in a basic and comprehensive format, using graphics and other visual tools. I talk about new emerging technologies such as Holographic Software and Artificial Intelligence and explain the Human Process and Machine Process of Computing open and available to the beginner and to seniors, just starting to understand the computing technologies.

Some of the hidden tools and resources, such as the use of Explorer Shell, and the Shell structure Utility and Resources built into Windows, like Perf Mon and Resmon, and others where the user can take advantage of this information to manage and troubleshoot their own machine and hardware devices. Built in utilities like CMD the command line and MMC Microsoft Management Console, that empowers the user to understand and manage both the hardware and software. I include in this book a large amount of Graphic representations of the Windows Structure and organization, that will help the user understand how everything is put together by just looking at the Graphics, without having to read a large amount of Text. I show and explain the uses of all the basic hidden tools, that are built in and the System Configurations and Security built-in that can be setup by the user, without the use of any external software applications or utilities.

The user can setup their own very secure Security using the built-in tools and software such as GPEDIT and SECPOL, and others.

I explain the use of special utilities that are free to obtain and install, and to keep and maintain the Computer Registry free and clean of Junk and other unwanted software. These utilities are free and when installed will keep the machine clean and maintain a very high performance throughout its shelf life.

DEDICATION

I would like to dedicate this book to my wife Sarah for all her support and to my daughters Sarah, Keren and Karina for their encouragement in writing all of my knowledge and putting it on paper for posterity.

To the Seniors of Shadow Mountain Senior Center, in Phoenix, Arizona for taking my Computer Classes and allowing me to teach them basic and advanced information to maintain and keep their computers.

For their friendship and the support of all the Staff and Management of the Center and the great support of Phillip and his Staff for all the great work they do to help us as Volunteers support the Seniors, and the Center, and to help me setup my classes.

Thank You.

CONTENTS

CHAPTER 1

The Basics

Understanding the Hardware first is very important as it will determine what kind of Software can run and be installed on the Computer.
The most important parts of the hardware are the CPU or Processor, the Memory or RAM and the Storage, or Hard Drive, usually the C:> drive.

Additional Storage is available now as a FlashDrive that the user can plug into one of several USB Ports on the Computer Hardware.
USB Ports are Universal Serial Buss Ports that facilitate the installation of many devices onto the Computer hardware such as Printers, Cameras and Mouse.
The CPU or processor is the heart of the computer and the best processors are made by INTEL.

The processor speed should be a 2.5 Ghz as a minimum, and recommended is 2.8Ghz to 3.2 or higher. And be INTEL Dual-Core processor i-5 as a minimum to i-9 for the higher end. The faster the processor, the better.

Processors below the speed of 2.0 GHz are not recommended, as they will be very very slow.

Some computers are being sold with processors of 1.5 and 1.8 Ghz.

The minimum Storage should be 1 Tb (terabyte) or higher.

Ports and Network Cards

The original Standard for the USB Ports were version 2.0 the new version for the USB Port is version 3.0, which make the transfer back and forth very fast; as compared to the old version 2.0 that was slow. Other hardware improvements are the new Standard for the internal Network Cards. The new Network Cards Standard is 802.11 /AC and AD

This allows the Network and (WI-FI) Wireless Networks, to run at Gigabit speeds; instead of the slower 100Mbps Ethernet Standard.

It is very important to have a very fast Network Cards in the Computer.
The Memory or RAM Random Access Memory used in Computers should be a minimum of 8 GB (Gigabytes).

BUILT IN ADMINISTRATIVE TOOLS

Administrative tools are built in Windows to allow the User and the System to Manage Operate and Setup Windows, and are available to the User from the Start menu or from Cortana.
The tools are: Component Services, Computer Management, Defragment and Optimize Drives, Disk Cleanup, Event Viewer, iSCSI Initiator, Local Security policy, ODBC Data Sources (32-bit and 64-bit), Performance Monitor, Print Management, Recovery Drive, Resource Monitor, Services, System Configuration, System Information, Task Scheduler,Windows Defender and Windows Memory Diagnostics.

BUILT IN WINDOWS SYSTEM TOOLS

The following System Tools are built into Windows and are available to users; **On Screen Keyboard**, to use the keyboard from the screen. **Phone** and **Phone Companion,** to link your Phone Contacts with your Computer or IPAD, and contains many other services available to the user. **System Information,** to display all the Hardware and Software running on your Computer and provides vital information about your system. **Uninstall,** to allow the user to uninstall any program application or utility running on the computer.

Windows Memory Diagnostic, will check the Memory on the user computer and detect any memory problems., and **Win Patrol Explorer** and **Win Patrol Help**, utilities running on Windows, and monitoring the system and user programs to make sure that they are working correctly. It will allow the user to disable bad startup programs affecting the computer performance.

HIDDEN DIAGNOSTIC TOOLS BUILT IN

These Diagnostic Tools are built into Windows and available to the User. 3D Builder, is an Application that allows the user to build and Draw 3D Models, of anything. Narrator will Read any text or steps the user takes when navigating the computer. It can read letters, emails and stories. Performance Monitor, is always Monitoring the Computer System Performance, this tool is available to the user at all times., Resource Monitor, is checking the uses and operation of all the System Hardware and Software Operations and uses of Resources such as Memory, Storage and CPU Power. Its a valuable tool for the user and available at all times. Run, is a tool that allows the user to execute any programs or utilities immediately, and is a powerful search and execute tool. System Configuration, provides information about the Windows System running on the user computer,the hardware and software Specs and many other useful information. Task Manager, perhaps the most important tool, that manages all of the active Windows Tasks running. It allows the user to stop any task that may be Frozen, and reset Windows. To call the Task Manager, just type CTRL ALT and DEL Keys together, and select Task Manager from the display window.

GETTING THE HIDDEN BATTERY REPORT IN WINDOWS 10, 7 and 8.___

The Status of the Computer Battery in the User Computer is available by typing a command into the **CMD** Command Line, to create the Report on the C:/ Drive. Two Modes can be used;

Mode 1. The Status of the Battery on the User Computer can be obtained using the **CMD** Command Line Utility built into Windows. Type CMD in the Startup Window in Windows, then make a shortcut of the CMD desktop App; right click on it and select" Run as Administrator" then type: powercfg /batteryreport /output "C:\battery_report.html" in the **C:/** command window, to create the file.

In Windows, goto your **C:/** Drive and look for the file; *battery_report* that was just created, to Print it or View it.

 Mode 2. Right-click on the **Start menu button** then choose **Command Prompt (Admin)**, then type: powercfg /batteryreport /output "C:\battery_report.html" into the new command window, press Enter., to create the Report on your C:/ Drive, so it can be printed or just to view it.

CHAPTER 2

"About Computers, with Graphic Layout."

We human Users are different from Machines (Computer Hardware) in many ways. Both Machines and Humans are governed by, we can call it; RULES , REGULATIONS and PROTOCOLS.

To find the Solution to a problem we can use our brains in various ways:

- We use CRITICAL THINKING
- LOGICAL THINKING
- CONDITIONAL THINKING
- ANALITICAL THINKING
- COMPARATIVE THINKING
- REASONING
  At the same time., to resolve a problem.

Machines, use "ANALITICAL Thinking", only;
  based on TASKs as
    Requested by the user. Computers are TASK
    DRIVEN Machines.

- Example of the new IBM Supercomputer
  and the Smart Engineer at Los Alamos,
  NM." Where is God" question.*

We must realize sometimes that we are asking
a "Machine" to give us information that we
want, not realizing that machines do not
"Think like us" and they have Hardware
Limitations.

We must never try to tell a machine "Computer" How to do its Job. As most machines operate under the Protocol "H" and humans use Protocol "W". which includes, the "Show me Protocol".

Protocol "H" is the "How to do" Protocol; used by machines, and How to use the "USER's GUIDE." and USER's MANUAL."
1. How to complete the Task
2. How to connect the Cables
3. How to Interface correctly with the User
4. How to Process the Information my User needs
5. How to use my Memory efficiently
6. How to Turn on my machine
7. How to Display my Desktop
8. How to Protect the machine from Viruses and other Malware.

Protocol "W" is the WHAT, WHEN, WHERE, WHY, WHO, WITH, WHICH, of what USERS should know, or ask the Computers to provide.

- Where do I go to get the information, I am looking for.?
- What do I do if my Computer "FREEZES" or get the "BLUE SCREEN OF DEATH"?
- What Utilities are available to me to Resolve my problem.
- Why is my Application not working.?
- When can I access my Data.?
- Who loaded this Application or Utility.? The System or the User.?
- Which Browser should I use.?
- With all the Tasks I am asking my Computer to do, will it work ok and correctly.?

Sometimes we are looking for Information in the wrong places, and assume that Computers can and will go to the correct place to find the information for us, (A Human Response); we forget the Limitations and did not give the Machine a clear Task to do. (We assume that the Computer knows where to go to find the information; even tough, we did not give it the correct Task, a WHERE to go, a WHAT we are looking for. (Does a Computer know that there is a PUBLIC DOMAIN location on the Internet?

Sometimes we need to THINK like Machines. Analytical Thinking. To convey to the Machine WHAT we Want and WHERE we want to go. Our requests will always need to be converted to Zero's and One's; the Machine Language.

Software.__

When we are looking for information on the INTERNET and we use a Computer with the necessary Software, we need to go to the correct Places on the INTERNET so that the Computer SOFTWARE can work to find the information we are looking for. Then the Question is; WHERE do we go.

What type of BROWSER should we use.? What kind of Search Engines should we use.? What kind of **Search Operators,** should we use? The Plus (+) or Minus (-) or Wild-Card (*.*) or AND-OR-NAND-NOT, etc.. to find what we want. Example; Search Cars NOT Vans., or   Search Trucks NOT Suv's.
A Natural Language Search Engine or
A Semantic Search Engine or just a Plain Standard Search Engine.
Using the correct Search Engine and Web Browser will enhance and facilitate our Search to find quickly what we are asking the computer to find.

Hardware. ___ **Minimum Hardware Requirements:**

1. **Processor**: Should be an INTEL processor, i-5, i-7, i-8 Dual or Quad-Core with a minimum speed of 2.5Ghz, or 2.8Ghz or 3.0Ghz or higher speed. Do not buy Computers with AMD Processors., they over-heat and require a fan.

2. **Memory:** Minimum RAM Memory should be 8GB-DDR3 or better, do not buy machines with 2GB or 3GB or 6GB of RAM Memory. RAM Memory is allocated in pairs of 1, 2, 4, 8, 16, 32, 64, and 128 GB; not in ODD numbers like; 3GB or 6GB. If the computer have 3Gb or 6GB; it means its **Sharing** its Memory with the **Display**; and leaving the Applications with very little Memory to work with.

3. **Storage:** Minimum Storage should be 1Tb. (Terabyte) or higher, internal or external. Machines with 500GB or more, is a waste of money and time.

4. **Ports:** Computers should have a minimum of 4 USB 2.0 Ports, one USB 3.0 and at least 1 or 2 HDMI Ports.

5. **DVD/CD** Player: Computers should have a Read/Write DVD/CD Player built into the hardware. CD/DVD R/W as a minimum., to facilitate **burning** a CD/DVD and be able to create and/or open an **ISO** File.

6. **Network:** The minimum Network Card should be 802.11 a/b/**AC** or **AD**. For Gigabit Wireless and/or Wired Ethernet Network. As a minimum, Gigabit Ethernet, using Dual Band Gigabit Routers.

7. **Operating System** (OS) : Minimum should be a 64 Bit Operating System for Windows or Macintosh.

8. **Best Battery**: for a Laptop; Battery should be a Polymer/Ceramic or Magnesium Battery and **not a** "Lithium-Ion ". However, most Computers come with Lithium-Ion Batteries; which are cheaper.

THE BASICS IN GRAPHICS . ____

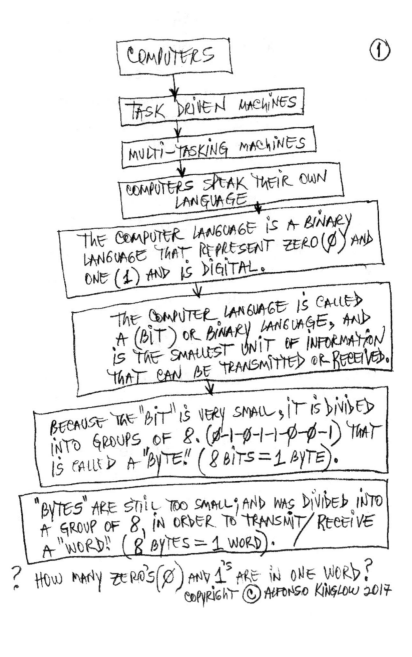

COMPUTERS

↓

TASK DRIVEN MACHINES

↓

MULTI-TASKING MACHINES

↓

COMPUTERS SPEAK THEIR OWN LANGUAGE

↓

THE COMPUTER LANGUAGE IS A BINARY LANGUAGE THAT REPRESENT ZERO ($\emptyset$) AND ONE (1) AND IS DIGITAL.

↓

THE COMPUTER LANGUAGE IS CALLED A (BIT) OR BINARY LANGUAGE, AND IS THE SMALLEST UNIT OF INFORMATION THAT CAN BE TRANSMITTED OR RECEIVED.

↓

BECAUSE THE "BIT" IS VERY SMALL, IT IS DIVIDED INTO GROUPS OF 8. ($\emptyset$-1-$\emptyset$-1-1-$\emptyset$-$\emptyset$-1) THAT IS CALLED A "BYTE!" (8 BITS = 1 BYTE).

"BYTES" ARE STILL TOO SMALL; AND WAS DIVIDED INTO A GROUP OF 8, IN ORDER TO TRANSMIT / RECEIVE A "WORD!" (8 BYTES = 1 WORD).

? HOW MANY ZERO'S ($\emptyset$) AND 1's ARE IN ONE WORD?

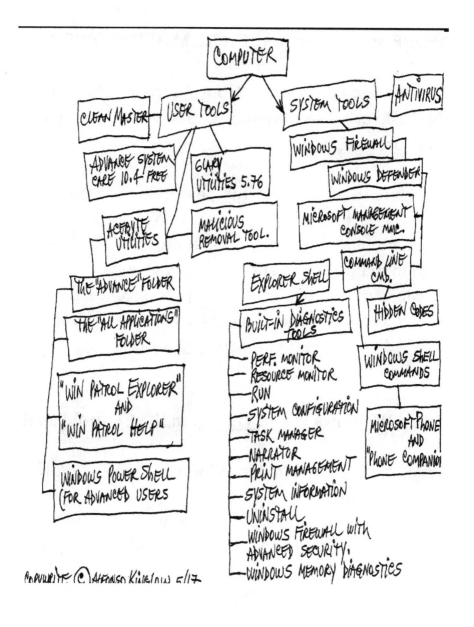

COMPUTER

CLEAN MASTER — USER TOOLS — SYSTEM TOOLS — ANTIVIRUS

ADVANCE SYSTEM CARE 10.4 FREE

GLARY UTILITIES 5.76

WINDOWS FIREWALL

WINDOWS DEFENDER

ACEBYTE UTILITIES

MALICIOUS REMOVAL TOOL.

MICROSOFT MANAGEMENT CONSOLE MMC.

COMMAND LINE CMD.

THE "ADVANCE" FOLDER

THE "ALL APPLICATIONS" FOLDER

EXPLORER SHELL

BUILT-IN DIAGNOSTICS TOOLS

HIDDEN CODES

"WIN PATROL EXPLORER" AND "WIN PATROL HELP"

WINDOWS POWER SHELL (FOR ADVANCED USERS

- PERF. MONITOR
- RESOURCE MONITOR
- RUN
- SYSTEM CONFIGURATION
- TASK MANAGER
- NARRATOR
- PRINT MANAGEMENT
- SYSTEM INFORMATION
- UNINSTALL
- WINDOWS FIREWALL WITH ADVANCED SECURITY.
- WINDOWS MEMORY DIAGNOSTICS

WINDOWS SHELL COMMANDS

MICROSOFT PHONE AND "PHONE COMPANION"

MORE PERFORMANCE FROM WINDOWS OS.

To get more Performance from Windows OS, open the Taskbar and type: **sysdm.cpl** into the search box. Next press <Enter>

Switch to the Advanced Tab, under the Performance, click the Settings button to disable Windows Animations, Fades, Font smoothing, drop shadows behind dialog boxes, and other visual enhancements that take up more memory and processor time.
To keep Windows as visually back as possible, click the "Adjust for Best Performance" Checkbox; Exit and Restart.

Setup Windows Power Option in the Control Panel.

Goto the **Control Panel** in Windows, open the Power Options App
Setup each of the Power Options like the handouts, they must be set to **Never, Never, Never** and **Do Nothing,** example like" When I close the lid"; Do Nothing..etc..

Change settings for the plan: Balanced
Choose the sleep and display settings that you want your computer to use.

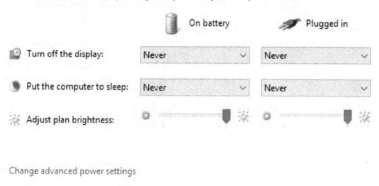

	On battery	Plugged in
Turn off the display:	Never	Never
Put the computer to sleep:	Never	Never
Adjust plan brightness:		

Change advanced power settings

Restore default settings for this plan

Next Setting:

Define power buttons and turn on password protection
Choose the power settings that you want for your computer. The changes you make to the settings on this page apply to all of your power plans.

Change settings that are currently unavailable

Power and sleep buttons and lid settings

	On battery	Plugged in
When I press the power button:	Shut down	Shut down
When I press the sleep button:	Do nothing	Do nothing
When I close the lid:	Do nothing	Do nothing

Shutdown settings

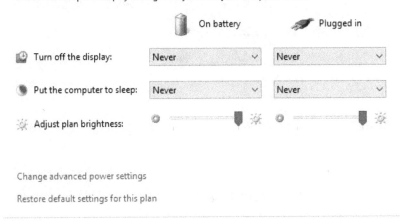

Change settings for the plan: Balanced

Choose the sleep and display settings that you want your computer to use.

	On battery	Plugged in
Turn off the display:	Never	Never
Put the computer to sleep:	Never	Never
Adjust plan brightness:		

Change advanced power settings

Restore default settings for this plan

CHAPTER THREE

How it all began. __

I began to develop a format for my books called .gbf or Graphics Box Format, where I use Graphics to Teach and explain Computer Technology to beginners and Users with some knowledge of Computers.

(gbf) Graphics Box Format, is in Review and could be the next Standard in Desktop Publishing, most of all my Graphics were design with No.2 pencil and Scanned as .PDF documents in high resolution.

The goal is for the student to look at the Graphic page and be able to identify the main components while putting them all together to convey a better understanding of the Technology, Students will then not necessarily have to read 3 of 5 pages of Text to understand what is going on and how the system works.

My Graphics are scanned at 300 to 600 dpi in high resolution, for easy reading. Information is broken down into graphics boxes with input and output links. These graphic boxes are active objects on the graphic pages, with Clear Text and are integrated into an algorithm to connect the graphics with holographic Software been developed, of which some are now available at the publication date of this book.

The Hololens and Holographic Scanner is been developed by Microsoft and will be available later on this year.
Graphic Box Format (.gbf) is been reviewed, and later will be able to Convert Graphics back to Text, in its original form.

For now it is my hope that the Graphics will clarify, expand and explain in a very simple and visual way how technology works, and facilitate the clear understanding of Computers for students as well as for advanced users.

Graphics is a visual tool used by Teachers and all Educators
to convey information rapidly and makes it easy to understand Concepts in Computer Technology.

My goal is to develop the graphics for it to be interactive and holographic so that it can be manipulated to expand the understanding of how text and graphic interact and can be connected to manipulate data, above the page.

Using my Convert program and algorithm, graphics in .gbf will be able to be converted back to text, and retain its original formatting.

Graphics Box Format is mentioned in my books " Not Just Another Computer Book Two" and also in "Not Just Another Computer Book For Advanced Users".

More information will be available later about this new Technology in my next book.

ONE
Concept Example of Graphics

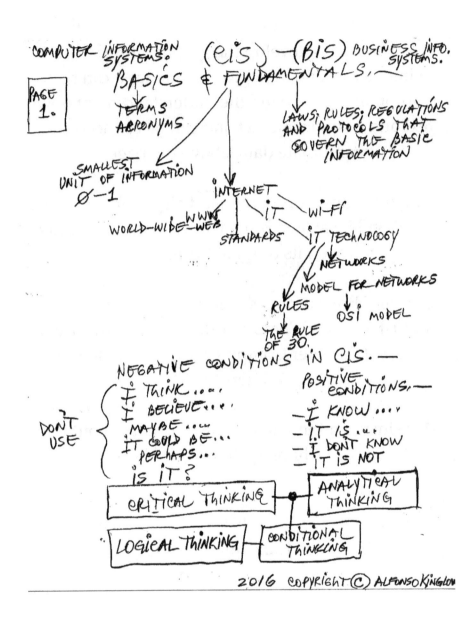

COMPUTER INFORMATION SYSTEMS: (CIS) — (BIS) BUSINESS INFO. SYSTEMS.

BASICS & FUNDAMENTALS,—

PAGE 1.

TERMS
ACRONYMS

LAWS; RULES; REGULATIONS AND PROTOCOLS THAT GOVERN THE BASIC INFORMATION

"SMALLEST UNIT OF INFORMATION
0 — 1

INTERNET
IT   WI-FI
WORLD-WIDE-WEB WWW
STANDARDS   IT TECHNOLOGY
NETWORKS
MODEL FOR NETWORKS
RULES   OSI MODEL
THE RULE OF 30.

NEGATIVE CONDITIONS IN CIS. —

I THINK....
I BELIEVE....
MAYBE....
IT COULD BE...
PERHAPS...
IS IT ?

DON'T USE

POSITIVE CONDITIONS, —

— I KNOW ....
— IT IS ....
— I DON'T KNOW
— IT IS NOT

CRITICAL THINKING   ANALYTICAL THINKING

LOGICAL THINKING   CONDITIONAL THINKING

WHAT CAN COMPUTERS DO. —

BASIC COMPUTERS CAN NOT, AND ARE NOT:

- DUMB TERMINALS
- GAME MACHINES
- JUST HARDWARE
- JUST SOFTWARE
- CAN NOT DIVIDE BY ZERO (0).
- NECESSARY MACHINES TO SOME PEOPLE.
- EMPTY BOXES WITH INPUT AND OUTPUT
- IMUNE TO SICKNESS OR INFECTIONS VIRUSES
- WILL NOT LAST FOREVER.
- SECURE ALL THE TIME.

CAN AND COMPUTERS ARE:

- TASK DRIVEN MACHINES
- ANALYTICAL
- ARE INTELLIGENT
- USE THEIR OWN LANGUAGE. (BINARY)
- UNDERSTANDS ENGLISH
- UNIVERSAL MACHINES
- HAVE MEMORY
- REMEMBERS
- FIRST LINE OF DEFENSE
- PART OF THE "GRID"
- FAST, EFFICIENT WHEN USED CORRECTLY.
- USE MOM & DAD
- USE SPYS TO COMMUNICATE/REPORT
- CAN TALK, SPEAK
- THEY GIVE ACCESS, RIGHTS, PRIVILEGE, AND PERMISSIONS.
- HAVE A UNIVERSAL PASSWORD. AMEN
- HAVE A UNIVERSAL "TEST USER"/WORD HELLO
- SECURE MACHINES WITH PROPER SOFTWARE.
- HAVE LOCK AND KEY
- HELP US TO BE MORE PRODUCTIVE.

CONTINUE ——→

Introduction to Windows Graphics
in GBF (Graphics Box Format) from Text.

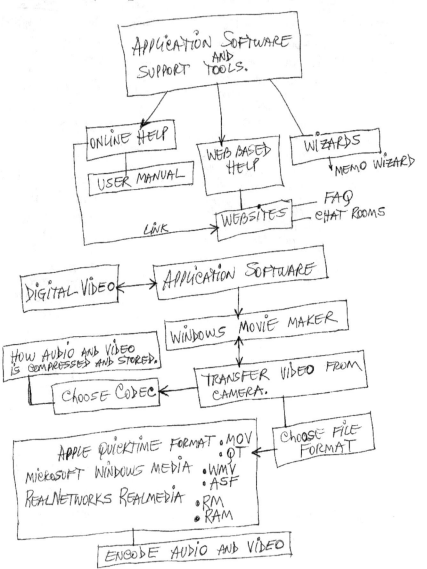

THE FIRST STANDARDS.—

- R-G-B = RED, GREEN, BLUE (SONY)
- C-M-Y-K = CYAN, MAGENTA, YELLOW, (K) CONSTANT (0-1)

- PANTONE CERTIFIED COLORS
- CROMALIN CERTIFIED COLORS (DUPONT)

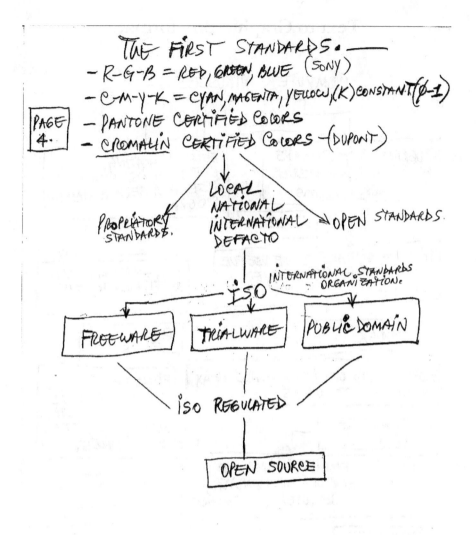

PROPRIETARY STANDARDS.

LOCAL
NATIONAL
INTERNATIONAL
DEFACTO

OPEN STANDARDS.

ISO   INTERNATIONAL STANDARDS ORGANIZATION.

FREEWARE   TRIALWARE   PUBLIC DOMAIN

ISO REGULATED

OPEN SOURCE

Text to Graphic Box format.

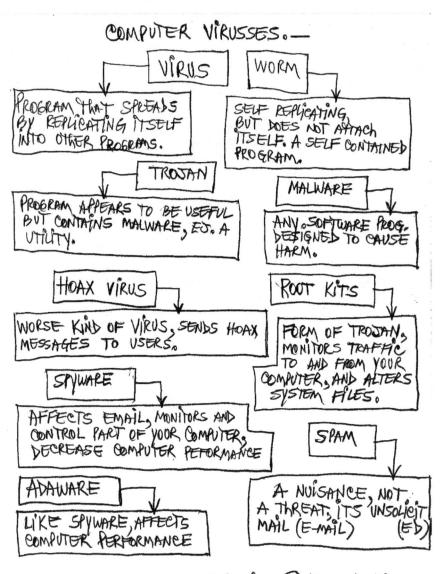

COMPUTER VIRUSSES.—

VIRUS

PROGRAM THAT SPREADS BY REPLICATING ITSELF INTO OTHER PROGRAMS.

WORM

SELF REPLICATING, BUT DOES NOT ATTACH ITSELF. A SELF CONTAINED PROGRAM.

TROJAN

PROGRAM APPEARS TO BE USEFUL BUT CONTAINS MALWARE, EJ. A UTILITY.

MALWARE

ANY SOFTWARE PROG. DESIGNED TO CAUSE HARM.

HOAX VIRUS

WORSE KIND OF VIRUS, SENDS HOAX MESSAGES TO USERS.

ROOT KITS

FORM OF TROJAN, MONITORS TRAFFIC TO AND FROM YOUR COMPUTER, AND ALTERS SYSTEM FILES.

SPYWARE

AFFECTS EMAIL, MONITORS AND CONTROL PART OF YOUR COMPUTER. DECREASE COMPUTER PEFORMANCE

SPAM

ADAWARE

LIKE SPYWARE, AFFECTS COMPUTER PERFORMANCE

A NUISANCE, NOT A THREAT, ITS UNSOLICIT MAIL (E-MAIL)   (ED)

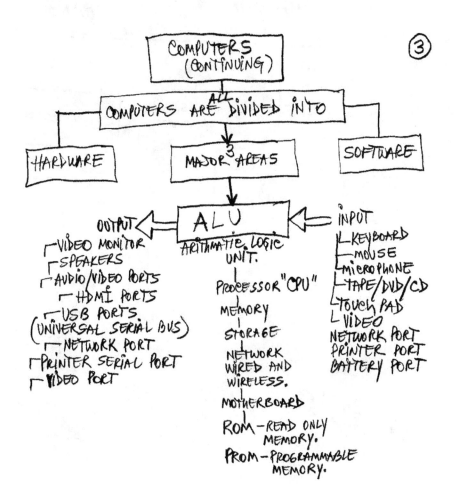

COMPUTERS
(CONTINUING)

③

COMPUTERS ARE ALL DIVIDED INTO

HARDWARE   MAJOR AREAS   SOFTWARE
                        3

OUTPUT ⟵ ALU ⟵ INPUT

ARITHMATIC LOGIC
UNIT.

OUTPUT
⌐VIDEO MONITOR
⌐SPEAKERS
⌐AUDIO/VIDEO PORTS
   ⌐HDMI PORTS
⌐USB PORTS.
(UNIVERSAL SERIAL BUS)
   ⌐NETWORK PORT
⌐PRINTER SERIAL PORT
⌐VIDEO PORT

PROCESSOR "CPU"

MEMORY

STORAGE

NETWORK
WIRED AND
WIRELESS.

MOTHERBOARD

ROM — READ ONLY
          MEMORY.

PROM — PROGRAMMABLE
            MEMORY.

INPUT
└KEYBOARD
⌐MOUSE
└MICROPHONE
└TAPE/DVD/CD
└TOUCH PAD
└VIDEO
NETWORK PORT
PRINTER PORT
BATTERY PORT

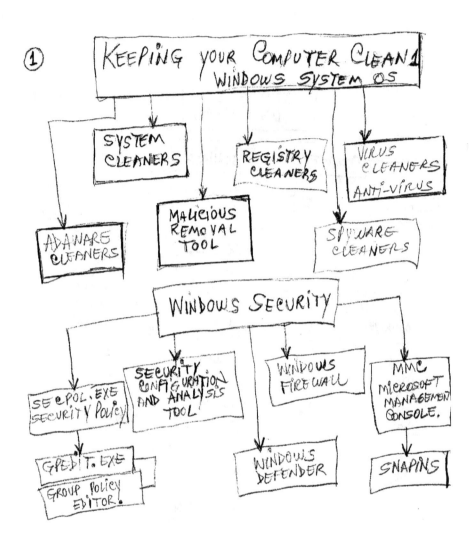

① KEEPING YOUR COMPUTER CLEAN
WINDOWS SYSTEM OS

SYSTEM CLEANERS

REGISTRY CLEANERS

VIRUS CLEANERS ANTI-VIRUS

ADAWARE CLEANERS

MALICIOUS REMOVAL TOOL

SPYWARE CLEANERS

WINDOWS SECURITY

SECURITY CONFIGURATION AND ANALYSIS TOOL

WINDOWS FIREWALL

MMC MICROSOFT MANAGEMENT CONSOLE.

SECPOL.EXE SECURITY POLICY

GPEDIT.EXE GROUP POLICY EDITOR.

WINDOWS DEFENDER

SNAPINS

INTERNET PROTOCOL AND THE WORLD WIDE WEB.—

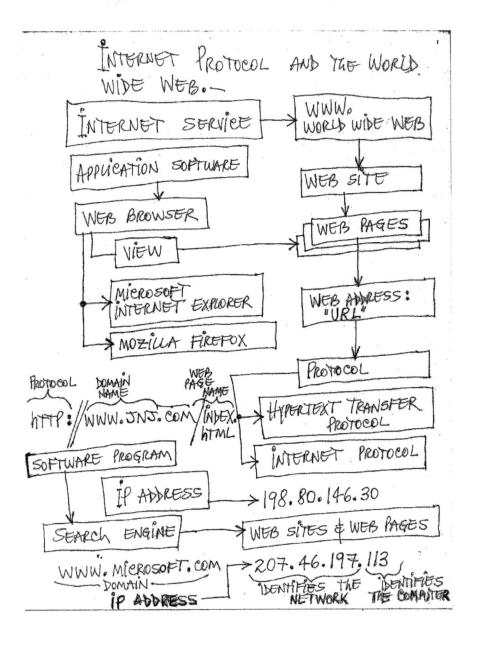

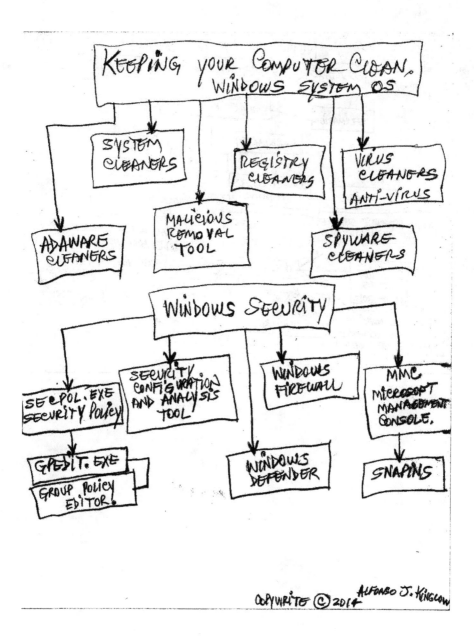

ALFONSO J. KINGLOW

NETWORKS AND THE INTERNET.

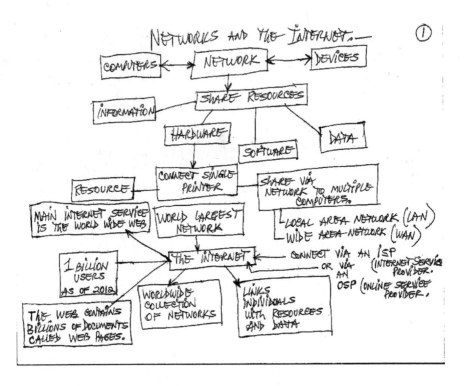

COMPUTERS ← NETWORK ← → DEVICES

NETWORK → SHARE RESOURCES

INFORMATION → SHARE RESOURCES

SHARE RESOURCES → HARDWARE, SOFTWARE, DATA

HARDWARE → CONNECT SINGLE PRINTER

RESOURCE → CONNECT SINGLE PRINTER

SHARE VIA NETWORK TO MULTIPLE COMPUTERS.
- LOCAL AREA NETWORK (LAN)
- WIDE AREA NETWORK (WAN)

MAIN INTERNET SERVICE IS THE WORLD WIDE WEB

WORLD LARGEST NETWORK

THE INTERNET

CONNECT VIA AN ISP (INTERNET SERVICE PROVIDER.
- OR VIA AN OSP (ONLINE SERVICE PROVIDER.

1 BILLION USERS AS OF 2012

WORLDWIDE COLLECTION OF NETWORKS

LINKS INDIVIDUALS WITH RESOURCES AND DATA

THE WEB CONTAINS BILLIONS OF DOCUMENTS CALLED WEB PAGES.

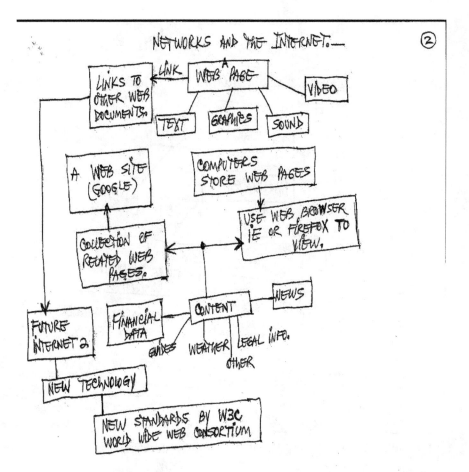

LINKS TO OTHER WEB DOCUMENTS.

LINK

WEB PAGE

VIDEO

TEXT

GRAPHICS

SOUND

A WEB SITE (GOOGLE)

COMPUTERS STORE WEB PAGES

USE WEB BROWSER IE OR FIREFOX TO VIEW.

COLLECTION OF RELATED WEB PAGES.

FUTURE INTERNET 2.

FINANCIAL DATA

CONTENT

NEWS

GUIDES

WEATHER

LEGAL INFO.

OTHER

NEW TECHNOLOGY

NEW STANDARDS BY W3C WORLD WIDE WEB CONSORTIUM

NETWORKS AND THE INTERNET.— ①

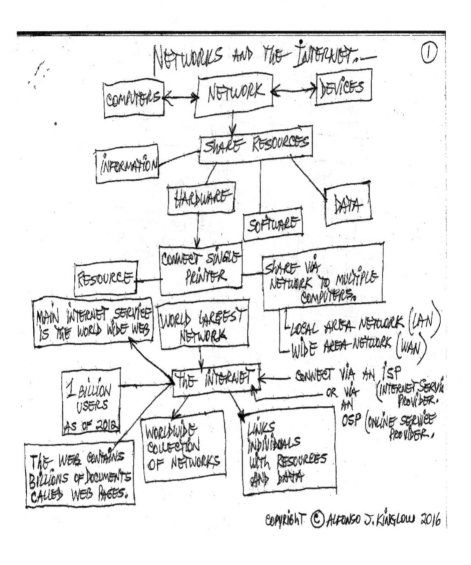

COMPUTERS ← → NETWORK ← → DEVICES

NETWORK → SHARE RESOURCES

INFORMATION

HARDWARE

SOFTWARE

DATA

CONNECT SINGLE PRINTER

RESOURCE

SHARE VIA NETWORK TO MULTIPLE COMPUTERS.

MAIN INTERNET SERVICE IS THE WORLD WIDE WEB

WORLD LARGEST NETWORK

└ LOCAL AREA NETWORK (LAN)
└ WIDE AREA NETWORK (WAN)

THE INTERNET ←

CONNECT VIA AN ISP (INTERNET SERVICE PROVIDER.
OR VIA AN OSP (ONLINE SERVICE PROVIDER.

1 BILLION USERS AS OF 2012

WORLDWIDE COLLECTION OF NETWORKS

LINKS INDIVIDUALS WITH RESOURCES AND DATA

THE WEB CONTAINS BILLIONS OF DOCUMENTS CALLED WEB PAGES.

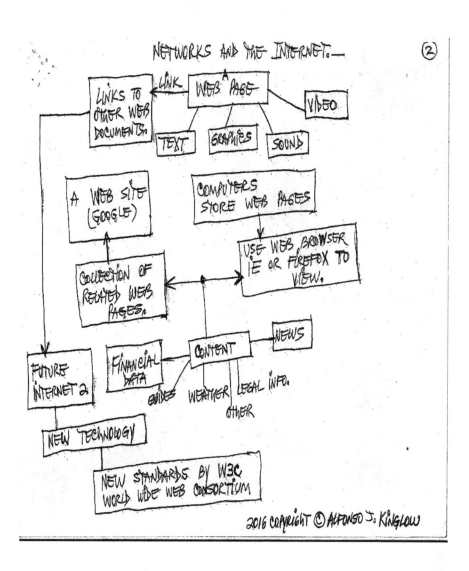

LINKS TO OTHER WEB DOCUMENTS.

LINK

WEB PAGE

VIDEO

TEXT

GRAPHICS

SOUND

A WEB SITE (GOOGLE)

COMPUTERS STORE WEB PAGES

USE WEB BROWSER IE OR FIREFOX TO VIEW.

COLLECTION OF RELATED WEB PAGES.

FUTURE INTERNET 2

FINANCIAL DATA

CONTENT

NEWS

GUIDES

WEATHER

LEGAL INFO.

OTHER

NEW TECHNOLOGY

NEW STANDARDS BY W3C WORLD WIDE WEB CONSORTIUM

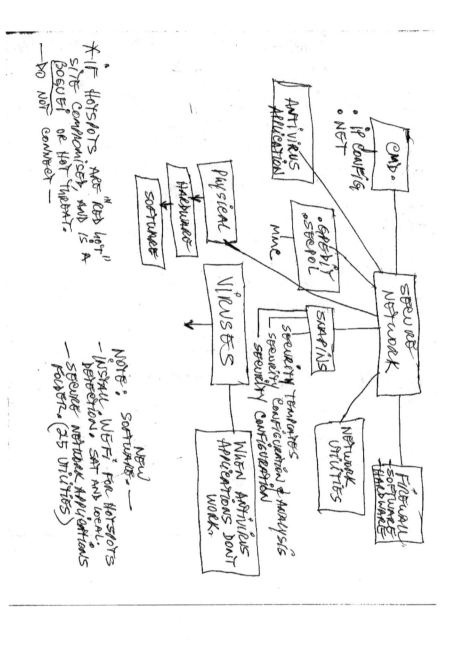

CMD:
• IP config
• NET

ANTIVIRUS APPLICATION

• GPEDIT
• SECPOL
MMC

PHYSICAL
  HARDWARE
  SOFTWARE

VIRUSES

SECURE NETWORK
  FIREWALL, SOFTWARE, HARDWARE
  NETWORK UTILITIES

SNAPINS
  SECURITY TEMPLATES
  SECURITY CONFIGURATION & ANALYSIS
  SECURITY CONFIGURATION

WHEN ANTIVIRUS APPLICATIONS DON'T WORK.

NOTE: SOFTWARE—
NEW
- INSTALL WIFI FOR HOTSPOTS
- DETECTION, SAT AND LOCAL.
- SECURE NETWORK APPLICATIONS FOLDER. (25 UTILITIES)

✱ IF HOTSPOTS ARE "RED HOT" SITE COMPROMISED, AND IS A ROGUE! OR HOT THREAT.
— DO NOT CONNECT —

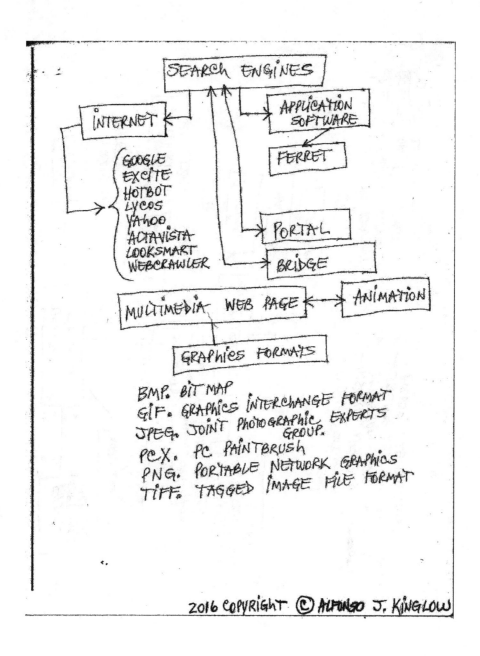

SEARCH ENGINES

INTERNET

APPLICATION SOFTWARE

FERRET

GOOGLE
EXCITE
HOTBOT
LYCOS
YAHOO
ALTAVISTA
LOOKSMART
WEBCRAWLER

PORTAL

BRIDGE

MULTIMEDIA WEB PAGE

ANIMATION

GRAPHICS FORMATS

BMP. BIT MAP
GIF. GRAPHICS INTERCHANGE FORMAT
JPEG. JOINT PHOTOGRAPHIC EXPERTS GROUP.
PCX. PC PAINTBRUSH
PNG. PORTABLE NETWORK GRAPHICS
TIFF. TAGGED IMAGE FILE FORMAT

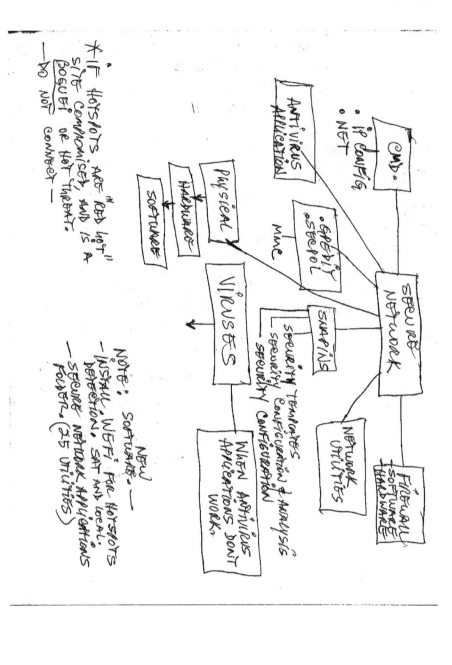

CMD:
• ip config
• net

ANTIVIRUS APPLICATION

SECURE NETWORK

SPECIFY
• STEP 01
MMC.

SECURITY TEMPLATES
SECURITY CONFIGURATION & ANALYSIS
SECURITY CONFIGURATION

SNAPINS

PHYSICAL
HARDWARE
SOFTWARE

VIRUSES

WHEN ANTIVIRUS APPLICATIONS DON'T WORK.

NETWORK UTILITIES

FIREWALL
SOFTWARE
HARDWARE

*IF HOTSPOTS ARE "RED HOT" SITE COMPROMISED, AND IS A BOGUS! OR HOT THREAT.
—DO NOT CONNECT—

NOTE: SOFTWARE—
NEW
—INSTALL WIFI FOR HOTSPOTS DETECTION. SAT AND LOCAL.
—SECURE NETWORK APPLICATIONS FOLDER. (25 UTILITIES)

SOFTWARE APPLICATIONS
AND
MULTIMEDIA SOFTWARE.

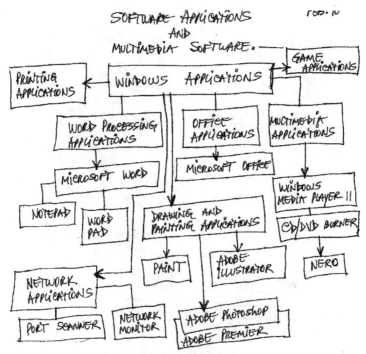

NOTE:

INSTALL APPLICATIONS VS. RUN APPLICATIONS
UNINSTALL APPLICATIONS VS. DELETE APPLICATIONS
ADD AND REMOVE APPLICATIONS (SOFTWARE)
UTILITY VS. APPLICATIONS
USER INSTALL VS. SYSTEM INSTALL APPLICATIONS

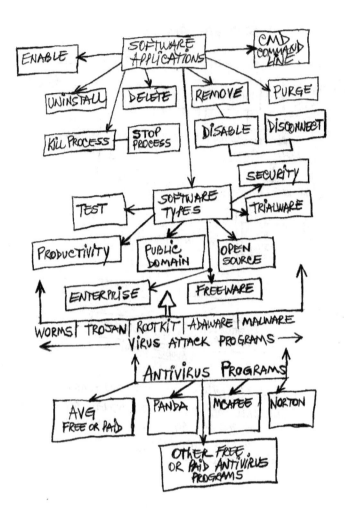

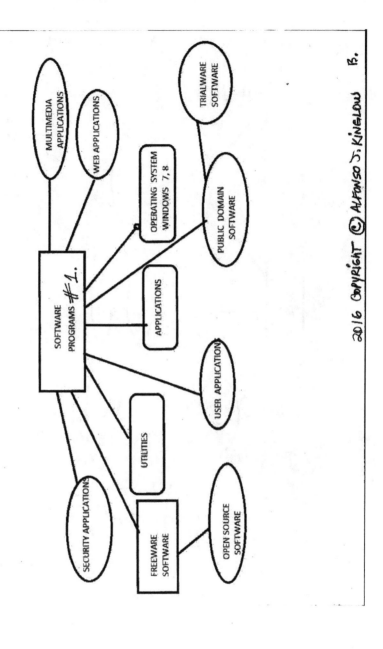

SOFTWARE PROGRAMS #1.

- MULTIMEDIA APPLICATIONS
- WEB APPLICATIONS
- OPERATING SYSTEM WINDOWS 7, 8
- TRIALWARE SOFTWARE
- PUBLIC DOMAIN SOFTWARE
- APPLICATIONS
- USER APPLICATION
- UTILITIES
- SECURITY APPLICATIONS
- FREEWARE SOFTWARE
- OPEN SOURCE SOFTWARE

13.

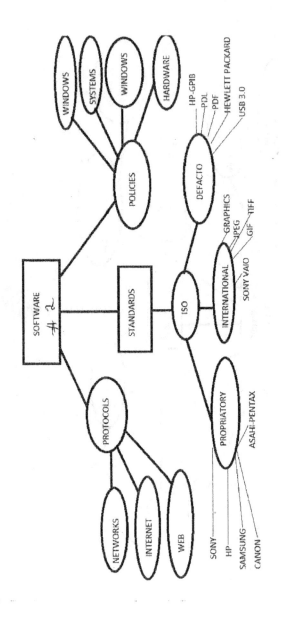

SOFTWARE #2

- PROTOCOLS
  - NETWORKS
  - INTERNET
  - WEB
- POLICIES
  - WINDOWS
  - SYSTEMS
  - WINDOWS
  - HARDWARE
- STANDARDS
  - ISO
    - DEFACTO
      - HP-GPIB
      - PDL
      - PDF
      - HEWLETT PACKARD
      - USB 3.0
    - INTERNATIONAL
      - GRAPHICS
      - JPEG
      - GIF
      - TIFF
      - SONY VAIO
    - PROPRIATORY
      - ASAHI-PENTAX
      - SONY
      - HP
      - SAMSUNG
      - CANON

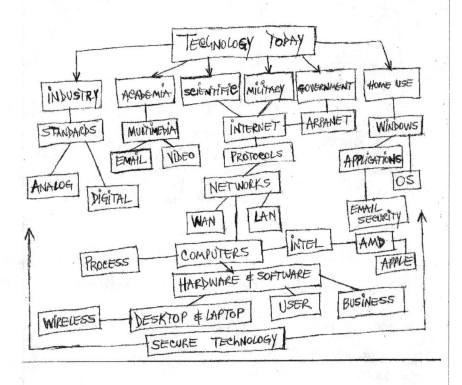

2016 COPYRIGHT © ALFONSO J. KINGLOW

THE INTERNET DOMAIN. —

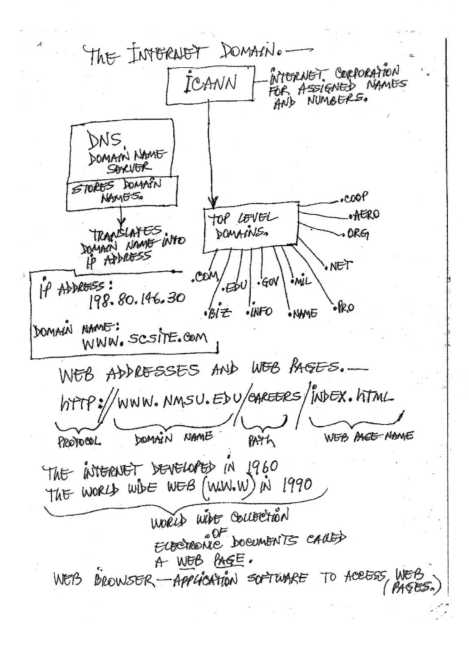

ICANN — INTERNET CORPORATION FOR ASSIGNED NAMES AND NUMBERS.

DNS. DOMAIN NAME SERVER
STORES DOMAIN NAMES.

TRANSLATES DOMAIN NAME INTO IP ADDRESS

TOP LEVEL DOMAINS.

.COOP
.AERO
.ORG
.NET
.COM
.EDU
.GOV
.MIL
.BIZ
.INFO
.NAME
.PRO

IP ADDRESS : 198. 80. 146. 30

DOMAIN NAME : WWW. SCSITE. COM

WEB ADDRESSES AND WEB PAGES. —

http://www. NMSU. EDU/CAREERS/INDEX. hTML

PROTOCOL   DOMAIN NAME   PATH   WEB PAGE NAME

THE INTERNET DEVELOPED IN 1960
THE WORLD WIDE WEB (W.W.W) IN 1990

WORLD WIDE COLLECTION OF
ELECTRONIC DOCUMENTS CALLED
A WEB PAGE.

WEB BROWSER — APPLICATION SOFTWARE TO ACCESS WEB (PAGES.)

ANALOG vs. DIGITAL.—

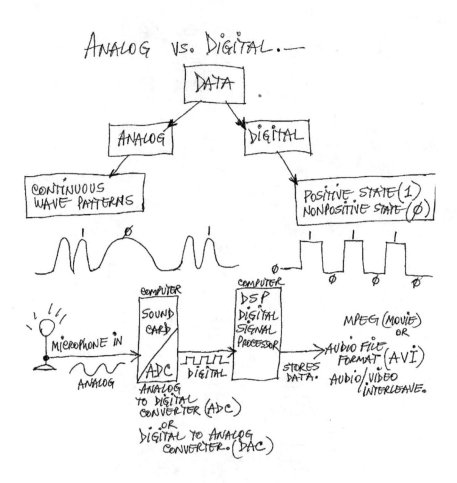

DATA

ANALOG → CONTINUOUS WAVE PATTERNS

DIGITAL → POSITIVE STATE (1) NONPOSITIVE STATE (∅)

MICROPHONE IN
ANALOG

COMPUTER
SOUND CARD
/ADC/
DIGITAL

ANALOG TO DIGITAL CONVERTER (ADC)
OR
DIGITAL TO ANALOG CONVERTER. (DAC)

COMPUTER
DSP
DIGITAL SIGNAL PROCESSOR

STORES DATA.

MPEG (MOVIE)
OR
AUDIO FILE FORMAT (AVI)
AUDIO/VIDEO INTERLEAVE.

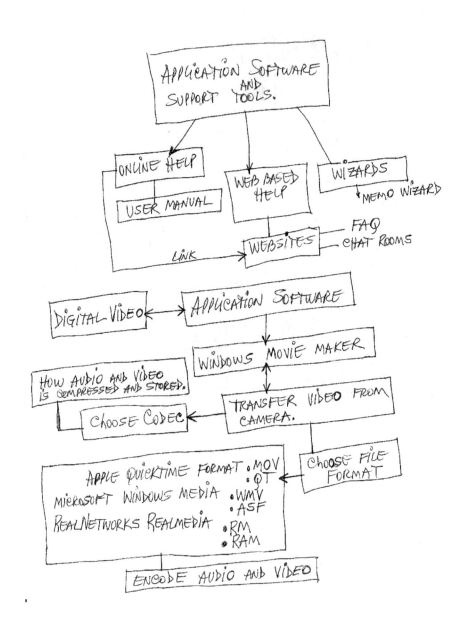

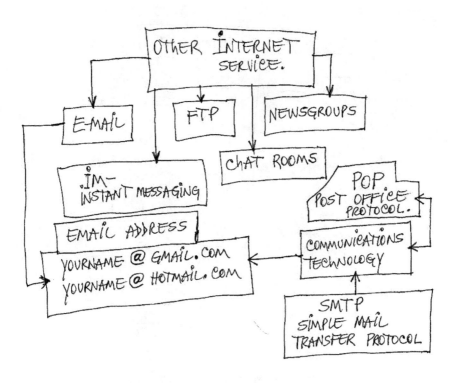

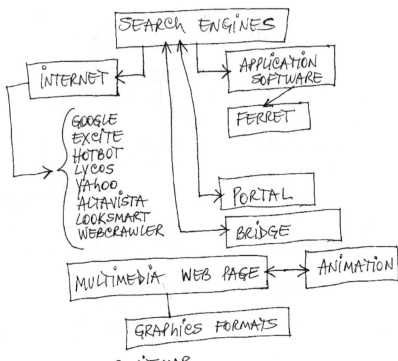

BMP. BITMAP
GIF. GRAPHICS INTERCHANGE FORMAT
JPEG. JOINT PHOTOGRAPHIC EXPERTS
                        GROUP.
PCX. PC PAINTBRUSH
PNG. PORTABLE NETWORK GRAPHICS
TIFF. TAGGED IMAGE FILE FORMAT

THE INTERNET AND THE WORLD WIDE WEB.
(WWW.)

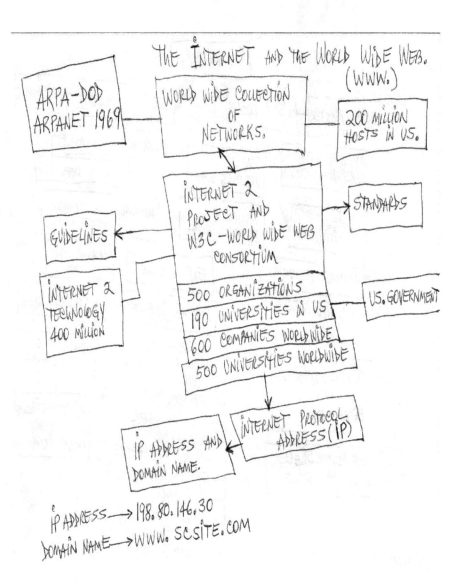

ARPA-DOD
ARPANET 1969

WORLD WIDE COLLECTION
OF
NETWORKS.

200 MILLION
HOSTS IN US.

INTERNET 2
PROJECT AND
W3C —WORLD WIDE WEB
CONSORTIUM

STANDARDS

GUIDELINES

INTERNET 2
TECHNOLOGY
400 MILLION

500 ORGANIZATIONS
190 UNIVERSITIES IN US
600 COMPANIES WORLDWIDE
500 UNIVERSITIES WORLDWIDE

U.S. GOVERNMENT

INTERNET PROTOCOL
ADDRESS (IP)

IP ADDRESS AND
DOMAIN NAME.

IP ADDRESS → 198. 80. 146. 30
DOMAIN NAME → WWW. SCSITE.COM

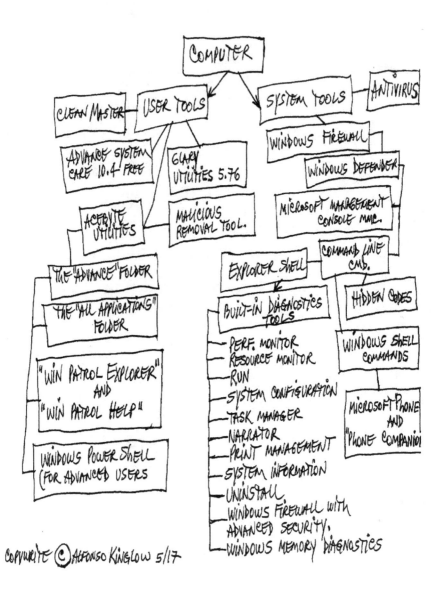

COPYWRITE © ALFONSO KINGLOW 5/17

Starting Windows 10 in Four Parts. ____

An Analysis of Windows 10 Presentation Parts.

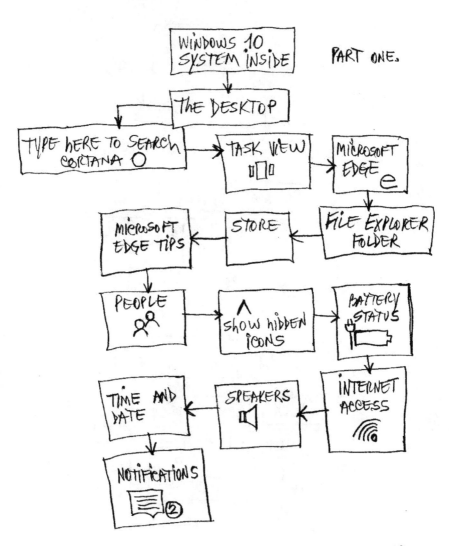

WINDOWS 10 SYSTEM INSIDE

PART ONE.

THE DESKTOP

TYPE HERE TO SEARCH CORTANA

TASK VIEW

MICROSOFT EDGE

MICROSOFT EDGE TIPS

STORE

FILE EXPLORER FOLDER

PEOPLE

SHOW HIDDEN ICONS

BATTERY STATUS

TIME AND DATE

SPEAKERS

INTERNET ACCESS

NOTIFICATIONS

PART TWO.

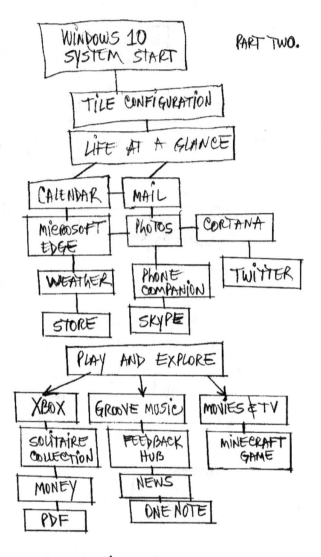

WINDOWS 10 SYSTEM START

TILE CONFIGURATION

LIFE AT A GLANCE

CALENDAR   MAIL

MICROSOFT EDGE   PHOTOS   CORTANA

WEATHER   PHONE COMPANION   TWITTER

STORE   SKYPE

PLAY AND EXPLORE

XBOX   GROOVE MUSIC   MOVIES & TV

SOLITAIRE COLLECTION   FEEDBACK HUB   MINECRAFT GAME

MONEY   NEWS

PDF   ONE NOTE

2018 COPYRIGHT © ALFONSO J. KINGLOW

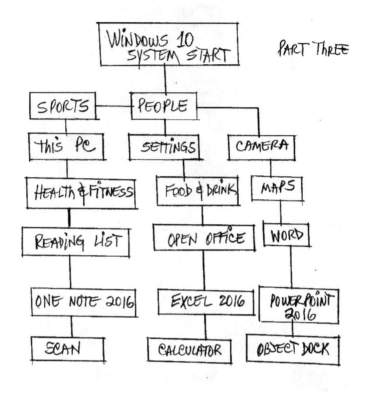

PART THREE

WINDOWS 10 SYSTEM START

SPORTS — PEOPLE

THIS PC

SETTINGS

CAMERA

HEALTH & FITNESS

FOOD & DRINK

MAPS

READING LIST

OPEN OFFICE

WORD

ONE NOTE 2016

EXCEL 2016

POWERPOINT 2016

SCAN

CALCULATOR

OBJECT DOCK

```
                    ┌─────────────────────┐
                    │ WINDOWS 10          │      PART FOUR
          ┌─────────│ SYSTEM START        │
          │         │ LEFT TILES          │
          │         └─────────────────────┘
          ▼
≡ RECENTLY ADDED

   ┌──────────────────────────┐
   │ SMART DEFRAG HOME        │
   └──────────────────────────┘
   ┌──────────────────────┐
   │ SMART DEFRAG 5       │
   └──────────────────────┘
   ┌────────────┐
   │ CD BURNER  │
   └────────────┘
         EXPAND/COLLAPSE

   MOST USED
   ┌───────────┐
   │ FIREFOX   │
   └───────────┘
   ┌────────────────────┐
   │ ACROBAT READER     │
   └────────────────────┘
   ┌────────────────────┐
   │ WINDOWS DEFENDER   │
   └────────────────────┘
   ┌──────────────┐
   │ 3D BUILDER   │
   └──────────────┘
   ┌────────────────┐
   │ AVG ANTIVIRUS  │
   └────────────────┘
   ┌──────────────────────────────────┐
   │ WINDOWS 10 UPGRADE ASSISTANCE    │
   └──────────────────────────────────┘
```

A - PROGRAMS IN ALPHABETICAL ORDER

TO

EXPLORER Z

OTHER ...→

SETTINGS

POWER

WINDOWS START KEY

2018 COPYRIGHT © ALFONSO KINGLOW

GETTING THE HIDDEN BATTERY REPORT IN WINDOWS 10, 7 AND 8.

Mode 1. The Status of the Battery on the User Computer can be obtained using the CMD Command Line Utility built into Windows. Type **CMD** in the Startup Window in Windows, then make a shortcut of the CMD desktop App; right click on it and select" Run as Administrator" then type: **powercfg /batteryreport /output "C:\battery_report.html"** in the **C:/** command window, to create the file. In Windows, goto your **C:/** Drive and look for the file; *battery_report* that was just created, to Print it or View it.

Mode 2. Right-click on the **Start menu button** then choose **Command Prompt (Admin)**, then type: **powercfg /batteryreport /output "C:\battery_report.html"** into the new command window, press Enter., to create the Report on your C:/ Drive, so it can be printed or just to view it.

Creating the All Applications Special Folder.

To create the all applications folder using the hidden embedded code in windows, create a blank folder and give it the name Applications, **put a period after the s.** and enter the following Code below.

**Start by using the "open bracket" {
enter the Code, and close the bracket }
and press <Enter>**

Applications.{4234d49b-0245-4df3-b780-3893943456e1}

enter.

The all applications folder will be created, this folder in windows will contain a lot of hidden graphics and graphics tools, you can use.

The Secret Advanced Folder. __

To create the Secret Advanced folder hidden in Windows, create a blank folder and call it Advanced. Put a period after the d. Open bracket {

Enter the Code, then close bracket }

Enter the following Code:

Advanced. { ED7BA470-8E54-465E-825C-99712043E01C}

<ENTER>

The Advanced folder will be created, which contains over 250 files to fix and troubleshoot Windows.

Content of Advanced Folder after its Creation.

Advanced

Advanced

Organize ▼

Name

∨ Administrative Tools (12)

Create and format hard disk partitions

Defragment and optimize your drives

Diagnose your computer's memory problems

Edit group policy

Free up disk space by deleting unnecessary files

Manage computer certificates

Schedule tasks

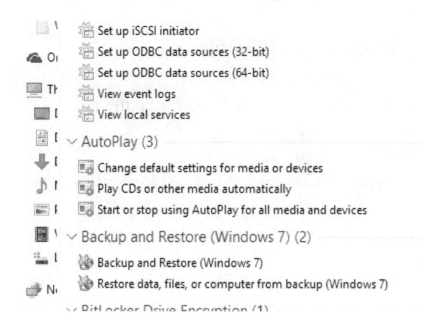

Set up iSCSI initiator

Set up ODBC data sources (32-bit)

Set up ODBC data sources (64-bit)

View event logs

View local services

∨ AutoPlay (3)

Change default settings for media or devices

Play CDs or other media automatically

Start or stop using AutoPlay for all media and devices

∨ Backup and Restore (Windows 7) (2)

Backup and Restore (Windows 7)

Restore data, files, or computer from backup (Windows 7)

∨ BitLocker Drive Encryption (1)

CHAPTER 4

WINDOWS BUILT IN DIAGNOSTIC TOOL. ____

Right- Click on the Windows Startup Icon, in the lower left side of the screen., to display the "RUN" command.

Type inside the RUN command: **DXDiag** and press <enter>

The Diagnostic program will start to run and check all of your machine. Follow the screens…

The Diagnostic tool will detect any problem your machine may have.

The Hidden Code(s) in Windows. ____

Window built in **Hidden Code** for Fixing and troubleshooting <u>all parts of your PC.</u>

Create the **Advanced. Folder:**

Then type the Code exactly, with **Open** and **Closed** Brackets like this { } and not [ ] .

Start:

a) Create a New Folder

b) Give it a name: **Advanced.**

c) Put a period after the d.

d) Enter the **Code** exactly:

   Advanced. {ED7BA470-8E54-465E-825C-99712043E01C}

<ENTER>

The new **green folder** will be created containing **237 files** with graphics showing the user **where, when**, and **why** to

Fix and Troubleshoot the computer.

Windows built in MMC (Microsoft Management Console. _

a) On the Startup or RUN command, type: MMC

The Microsoft Management Console window
will be displayed.
b) Create " **SNAPIN's** to manage your
Computer.

CHAPTER FIVE

Installed Software on new Computers

Most computers will already have the Software OS
such as Windows 7, 8 or 10, already installed with
some User Software. Most of the User Software will
be Trialware, there will be some free Games and
Utilities installed.
Trialware software will only have limited capabilities
and will only work for a period of 30 to 60 days
sometimes, some Trialware software do not install
the complete version of the software and only a basic
portion is installed, after the trial time; the user will
be required to purchase a license to install the full
version of the software. The Trialware version will
then have to be un-installed correctly in order to
remove it safely from your computer before you can
install the full license version of the software.

It is recommended that you install a full version of the software you want to use and not install Trialware software on your computer. Your computer may also come with a Trialware version of some kind of Antivirus software.

It is very important to note that the Trialware version of the Antivirus program will not fully protect your computer. After a short period of time you will also be required to purchase a full version of the Antivirus program.

You may install in the mean time a Free version of any Antivirus program; such as (.AVG) which is a Freeware Application. This will provide some Basic protection to your system, until you can install a complete Antivirus program.

The Free AVG Antivirus is a complete antivirus application, with the basic necessary modules to protect your computer. You may purchase the full application at any time which will give you more capabilities and protection. It is better to install Freeware Applications than any Trialware Application. You may also find many Public Domain Software that are very useful and are also free.

If you are looking for applications and utilities for your computer, you may find useful software in Public Domain, Open Source, and Freeware Software on the Internet. All these categories contain software that are free to use and download, and are not " Trialware".

Recommended for Windows 7, 8 and 10

The recommended Software OS should be the Basic standard version or the Professional version of the software. Windows 8 or 10 Professional is far better than Windows 8 or 10, Home, Student or Basic editions. Windows 8 and 10 operates in 32 bit mode or 64 bit mode. Sixty four (64 Bit) mode is faster and is recommended if you are going to use more than 4 Gb of Ram Memory. Windows 8 and 10 in 32 bit mode works just fine if you have 4 Gb of Ram Memory or higher. The more memory, the better. Eight (8GB) is recommended for Windows 10.

New users to Windows 8 and Windows 10, will notice that the OS does not have a START button. If you would like to have a Start button, because you are familiar with this capability from previous versions, you may install one.

The Windows 8 Start button is a free application that is available on the Internet, if you have Windows 10, then you do not need to use it., other free applications are also available for download at several web sites. You may do a Search on Freeware Software and Public Domain Software to get these applications and or utilities.

Almost all of the free applications and or utilities provided on a CD that is available from the Author of this book will work with Windows 7 and or Windows 8. It is recommended that you upgrade your computer to Windows 8. The new Windows 8.1 Upgrade removed the Start button and other basic components from the Desktop. It is recommended that you stay with Windows 8 until the new Windows 9 is released. Since very soon Windows 9 will be coming out, it will require some review. The Windows Operating System is evolving very quickly to provide the users with better and faster technologies.

Please note that we the users are the one's that are driving the technology, we are demanding better and faster hardware and software. We want more and faster applications and multimedia software. Large Software companies such as Microsoft Corporation, and other's; are trying to keep up with the user's demands.

We are now using more social media applications to communicate via the internet, such as Facebook and Twitter, and these companies are also trying to keep up with the user's demands.
Computers are now a necessity and are required in every household in America and elsewhere, as a very essential tool for business and or entertainment.

The speed of your computer will depend on the type of processor in your computer, with the amount of Ram Memory installed.
INTEL is the largest manufacturer of Computer Chips and Computer processors in the World, followed by AMD and others.

Intel Dual-Core Processors i-5, to i-7 and i-9 are very fast processors and are now available in some laptops and desktops computers. It is recommended that you get a Computer with one of these processors, with a Storage capacity of at least 1 Tb. (terabyte) minimum, up to 1.5 Tb. Or higher on Internal hard drive on some computers.

ABOUT THE NEW ATEVON DELUXE HDMI CABLE. ___

Latest version HDMI Cable supports **3D Content** and 4K@ **50/60hz Video, up to 18GBps bandwidth, 24k Gold Contacts** ensures ultimate video up to 32 Audio channels up to 1536 Khz audio sample frequency for highest audio fidelity, supports **48 Bit Deep Color, and 21.9 video aspect ratio.**
HDCP Compliant and **True HD-Dolby 7.1**

Connects all Blue-Ray & DVD Players and Computers with **HDMI output to 4K UHD TV,** Displays and all HD Audio Video devices.
Backward Compatible with HDMI Vers 2.0, v1.4 & 1.3

http://www.atevon.com/support

CHAPTER SIX

What you should know about "The Bit" and your Computer Processor Speed.__

The smallest unit of information that can be transmitted over the internet or to and from your computer is called a Bit.
The Bit is a binary number that represents 0 (zero) or 1 (one).
Using just these two numerical characters you can transmit any message you want to a computer since every letter in the alphabet has a binary equivalent sets of numbers, representing 8 bits.; such as 01100111. Since bits are very small they had to be divided and organized to handle large amounts of **Data** to facilitate **Storage** and distribution.

So, 8 Bits is equal to *1 Byte* and 8 Bytes is equal to *1 Word* . The following terms are therefore used in all Computers to designate thousands and millions of Bytes: *Kilo-bytes* is equal to one thousand bytes, *Mega-Bytes* is equal to 1 Million bytes, *Giga-bytes* is equal to 1 Trillion Bytes, *Tera-bytes* is equal to 1 Billion Bytes, etc.. These values are used in computers for storage and to designate computer memoryIn the case of designating Processor speeds, a different term is used to represent cycles per second or (cps) which is also designated in hertz, used in the name of the German Physicist that discovered it. So we say that processor speeds are measured in cycles per second or (cps) or we can also say in hertz or (hz).The speed of processors are always in Giga-hertz or Giga-cycles per second (Ghz). A fast processor should be above 2.0 Ghz per second. Anything below 2.0Ghz will be very slow. A processor speed above 2.0Ghz will be very fast. Fast computers have processors that are 2.5 Ghz to 3.0Ghz or higher., To achieve very fast speeds, processors are built with Dual-Core, which will have more that one processors. Some computer manufacturers chips will contain dual core processors running seven (7) or more processors and are designated with the "I" Code, such as Intel Processor Dual-Core i-7. To get a fast computer, make sure you meet the above requirements of a fast Processor and a very large storage for your data. Most computers will have at least a storage hard drive of at least 500 Gb (Giga-bytes) of storage or higher. You can now buy external hard drives for storage in the tera-byte range. In designating computer memory, a division was selected to facilitate operation and distribution of in line memory modules that were single or dual so thay could be used in various types of computers. These memory modules were called (SIMM's) or single in-line memory modules, and (DIMM's) Dual in-line memory modules, and Random access memory or (RAM). Memory used in computers were divided as 1, 2, 4, 8, 16, 32, 64 Gb (Giga bytes) of Ram memory or higher, always EVEN MULTIPLE numbers to meet computer standards. Computers with ODD MULTIPLE numbers are not acceptable, because the computer memory is shared with other parts of the computer such as the Video Display, not leaving enough memory for the system and or applications, and may not fully meet US or International Standards. Such computers are sold with 3 Gb of RAM memory or 6Gb of RAM memory; and are unacceptable.

How Computers are Divided. ___

Computers in general are divided into two parts,
Hardware and Software. Hardware contains all
the major parts of the computer such as the hard
drives, The CD/DVD drives, the processors,
memory and all the computer input

ports such as Printer port, USB port, video port,
and keyboard and mouse.
The computer hardware depends on the installed
memory, storage drive and processor speed
necessary to work with the Windows OS
Operating System.

With the hardware and the Windows OS also is
important to note the Accessories. Some of these
Accessories are built-into the Hardware and
Software. Some of the most important Hardware
utilities that are built-in are:
Hardware Security utility; Hardware
Management, part of the hardware management
is the Command Line CMD.
The hardware System Utilities that includes The
Firewall and
Defrag, and the User Utilities that contains the
Notepad,

WordPad and others.

The Hardware Security Utility contains the MMC and the hardware Snap-Ins., one of the most important utility built in to allow the user to manage and setup the Security and Configuration of the Computer.

The most important ports on your computer are; the USB ports, most computers will have 2 or more USB ports. USB is a standard that replaces the old computer ports that required large and cumbersome connectors and were very slow sending data back and forth to your computer. USB 2.0 became a defacto standard and was implemented several years ago into every computer hardware. It is very fast sending and receiving data. A USB cable which is thin with the flat USB connector is required to connect almost any device you wish to connect to your computer and it includes cameras, keyboards, Web cams, mouse, etc..
A new USB standard was released last year, its USB 3.0 which is faster than USB2.0 and almost all new computers now have this standard implemented into the hardware. It requires a USB 3.0 cable which is downward compatible to USB2.0

Software Defined

Software are the Programs that make all of the Hardware work. The major software in any computer system will be the OS or Operating System such as Windows. The other major software will be the Applications and Utilities. Some software will need to be installed by the user and some will be installed by the OS or Operating System. Major user software will be the Applications such as Microsoft Office, and others that will facilitate the users to become more productive. Utilities will protect the computer from threats and viruses.

Software programs in general are divided into the following areas: Software Applications, Productivity, Games, Development, Multimedia, Educational, Utilities, System, LAN Local Area Networks, Web Software, Maintenance, Network, Paint, Accessories, Programming, Basic, Communications, Cloud Software, WAN Wide Area Network (The Internet), Graphics, Antivirus, etc...

Software programs are Installed, Deleted, Removed, and Purged.

When a Software program is Installed, it must be Un-Installed.

When a software program is Deleted, it must be Un-Deleted.

To correctly remove Software Programs, it must be done in the Control Panel in Programs and Features, if you are running Windows 8. The program is then Uninstalled or Changed. Dragging a program to the Trash or Recycle Bin does not Remove it, to Remove a program it must be Shredded in the Recycle Bin.

To Destroy a program it must be Purged.

Most Software are in the following modes, Virtual Software, Hyper-V Software, Free Software, Search Software, Shared Software, Open Source Software, Public Domain Software, License Software, Encrypted Software, Decrypted Software, Cipher Software, Network Card Test Software or (loop back address Software), OS Windows Software(Operating Systems); Firewall Software, Security Software(Bit Locker), Printer Software, Email Software, DSL Router Software, etc..

Software Languages and Standards. __

Most Software are written in the following computer languages: Hypertext, used in Web Browsers on the Internet, Unix, Basic, Ada, C and C++ (C Plus Plus), Html (Hypertext Markup Language), Xml   (Extensible Markup Language), Fortran, Pascal, and High Level Compilers, etc....

The Standards that govern Software are: Defacto Standards, IEEE Project 802.x, The OSI Model and the ISO (International Standards Organization).

The Seven Pillars to Execute Software Programs.__

- Setup and Install the Software
- Uninstall and Undelete
- Add and Remove
- User Install and System Install
- Run, Search and Delete
- Free, Trial and Test
- Open Source and Public Domain software access

Search Software Formats. __

The following Search Software Formats are used on the Internet as follows:

Search with --------◎ AND or + -------◎ Red Cars and
Red Vans.   Green Apples + Red Apples.
Search with -------◎ OR ----------◎ One word to be in
search (Flight Attendant OR Stewardess)

Search with ------◎ AND NOT (-) -◎ suv AND NOT
auto (suv – auto)
Search with ----◎ Phrase Searching --◎ Exact Phrase
with " Harry Potter" Quotation.
 Search with ----◎ Wildcard ---◎ WRIT* CLOU* -◎
The Asterisk at the end of words.

Hardware.__

The Hardware is the box or frame that contains
all the major parts of a computer, the internal
hard drive, the CD/DVD Player, the different
input ports, the keyboard and mouse, the
processor and ram memory, the Ethernet
network card, the Wireless network card, the
video display, the LCD display(on laptops), the
sound card, the internal built in camera, the
internal microphone, etc.. One of the major Ports
is the USB (Universal Serial Bus) that is now used
to connect Printers, Cameras and multiple other
devices to your computer hardware.

Policies are built into the computer hardware to allow for security and to manage the hardware. Some of the most important policies are the SECPOL. MSC (Security Policy) and GPEDIT.

MSC (Group Policy Editor) these policies allow you to setup the security configuration on your computer hardware. These policies are launched using the Command Line (CMD) built into your computer, or by typing the policy directly into the START or RUN line. The Command Line CMD is provided as a means of accessing your Computer Hardware and Software policies and to directly manage a great part of your computer hardware, without requiring any software to manage policies.

It is used also for direct maintenance of the computer and comes with a reasonable help file. This file contains all of the commands used with the CMD. The command line window when launched appears with a black background. The background and text colors can be changed from a menu of different colors as well as the text size and window size.

Some preferred combinations are; red background with yellow text color or green background with white or purple text color, etc... To change the color background and text, click on the cmd icon in the upper left side of the command window.

To access all of the standard policies to set up your computer hardware you can find them in the MMC (Microsoft Management Console) built into your computer hardware.

The MMC allow the user to create SNAP-IN's to setup the hardware and security configuration. To access the MMC just type it into the CMD window or directly into the START or RUN line, on the lower left side of your computer.

CHAPTER SEVEN

Your Computer hardware Ports and your Desktop. ___

Most computers will have the following standard hardware ports; a printer port, the CD/DVD port, the mouse and keyboard ports, the microphone and audio ports, at least three to four USB ports, the video port, the Ethernet port, the power input port. The USB ports will serve as external ports to connect multiple devices, such as an external Hard Drive or external camera or Webcam.

Your computer hardware ports have *designated hardware symbols* to identify each port. A list of these hardware symbols are contained in this book. Each symbol is imprinted on the external hardware case to identify the port. These symbols meet international standards for hardware identification ports and some have become " *defacto standards.*"

The Desktop. ____

Your Desktop is one of the most important parts of your computer. When you turn on your computer it will boot up and display your desktop window. Your desktop will have a background color or image that can be changed by the user. Your desktop can get corrupted and it is very important to keep your desktop clean from clutter. Having many icons on your desktop will create clutter and take up storage space.

Protected Folders on your Computer.____

Special folders were created to keep your user documents and personal files, in order to keep them organized and off your desktop.
Such folders that are protected are: The *Documents folder*, the *Music folder*, the *Pictures folder*, and the *Videos folder*.

Some icons are required to be on your desktop so that they can be accessible immediately by the user and the system, such as: *My Computer, My Network* and *Internet Explorer* or IE.

If you need to put a copy of documents, pictures or other files you use daily, then you should put them into folders, if they are going to reside on your desktop; and not leave the icon open on your desktop. You could also create " *shortcuts* " of your documents and or applications or any other files you wish to leave on your desktop, instead of leaving the original document or image.

Shortcuts do not take up a lot of space or memory. Your desktop icons can be changed in the Control Panel in " *Personalization."*

SETUP A RESTORE POINT IN WINDOWS 10

To Setup a Restore Point and Turn on System protection in Windows:
Goto the Search box and type " **restore point**" in the Windows Search box.
Launch " Create a restore point" from the results select the restore point on computer system drive C:/ system

Select the system drive and click **Configure.**
Toggle Restore Settings to" Turn on system protection" set the maximum drive moving the slider and click ok. Leave 2 or 3 percent for restore points.

Click Create to create an initial restore point right away.

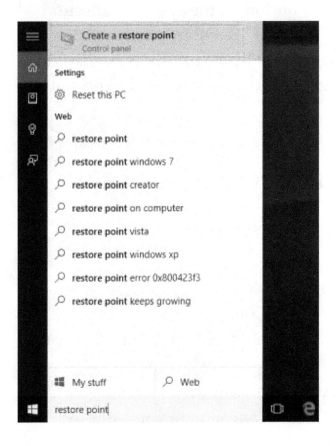

Name the initial restore point when prompted. Click Close when it is done.

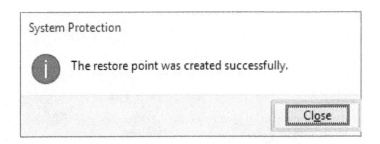

If you need to restore from one of these points, click the system restore button on the system protection tab. You can go to SAFE MODE by pressing F8 or Shift +F8 during boot as the computer is starting, to get to the emergency menu, to restore the computer.

TRACEROUTE AND PING UTILITIES FOR TESTING WINDOWS ADAPTERS AND NETWORK.____

Tool for testing Connectivity:

Type **CMD** or from RUN type CMD,   the command line., then

Type **tracert domain.com**

 To measure the delay connecting to any site.. or
 Trace the Network Path

Tracert nmsu.edu or

Tracert asu.edu   As Examples.

_____

  TEST YOUR NETWORK CARD.____

Use the command " PING " to perform a Loopback Test to check the Network Adapter on the Computer.

Use the command: PING
To test Network Card with **Loopback Test.**
Type CMD, and from the CMD Window type:
Ping 127.0.0.1

Using Explorer Shell Tool in Windows.

EXPLORER SHELL.

TO CREATE A PORTABLE FOLDER OF ANY PART OF WINDOWS SYSTEM.__

USING " EXPLORER SHELL"

Create a Short Cut Folder by selecting NEW and
    Shortcut
 In the shortcut window: **Type: Explorer Shell:** and
    the name of the Part of
Windows you want to create: for Example:

Explorer Shell:ControlPanelFolder   and
click NEXT
        another window will be displayed.
        Type the name you want to give to the folder,
and press <Finish>
        The new folder will be created.

Another Example: **Explorer Shell:AppsFolder**

This folder will be portable and can be used on any
    Windows Computer.

First you'll need to create a new shortcut. To do this, right-click on Desktop and select "**New -> Shortcut**": then type explorer shell: and type the name of the tool you want to create: IE: **explorer shell:ControlPanelFolder**

You can use any of following commands to create the desired shortcut:

explorer shell:MyComputerFolder (for My Computer shortcut)

explorer shell:RecycleBinFolder (for Recycle Bin shortcut)

explorer shell:ControlPanelFolder (for Control Panel shortcut)

explorer shell:Administrative Tools (for Administrative Tools shortcut)

explorer shell:ChangeRemoveProgramsFolder (for Programs and Features shortcut)

explorer shell:NetworkPlacesFolder (for Network shortcut)

explorer shell:Favorites (for Favorites shortcut)

explorer shell:HomegroupFolder (for Homegroup shortcut)

explorer shell:Games (for Games shortcut)

explorer shell:Fonts (for Fonts shortcut)

explorer shell:UserProfiles (for Users folder shortcut)

explorer shell:Profile (for your username folder shortcut)

explorer shell:Public (for Public folder shortcut)

explorer shell:My Documents (for Documents shortcut)

explorer shell:Common Documents (for

Public Documents shortcut)

explorer shell:My Music (for Music folder shortcut)

explorer shell:CommonMusic (for Public Music folder shortcut)

explorer shell:My Pictures (for Pictures folder shortcut)

explorer shell:CommonPictures (for Public Pictures folder shortcut)

explorer shell:My Video (for Videos folder shortcut)

explorer shell:CommonVideo (for Public Videos folder shortcut)

explorer shell:Downloads (for Downloads folder shortcut)

explorer shell:CommonDownloads (for Public Downloads folder shortcut)

explorer shell:::{3080F90E-D7AD-11D9-BD98-0000947B0257} (for Flip 3D or Window Switcher shortcut)

Here is a list of the Shell Commands:

WINDOWS SHELL COMMANDS.__

Shell Command	Description
shell:AccountPictures	Account Pictures

shell:AddNewProgramsFolder   The "Get Programs" Control panel item

shell:Administrative Tools   Administrative Tools

shell:AppData   Same as %appdata%, the c:\user\<username>\appdata\roaming folder

shell:Application Shortcuts   Opens the folder which stores all Modern apps shortcuts

shell:AppsFolder   The virtual folder which stores all installed Modern apps

shell:AppUpdatesFolder   The "Installed Updates" Control panel item

shell:Cache   IE's cache folder (Temporary Internet Files)

shell:CD Burning   Temporary Burn Folder

shell:ChangeRemoveProgramsFolder   The "Uninstall a program" Control panel item

shell:Common Administrative Tools   The Administrative Tools folder for all users

shell:Common AppData   The C:\ProgramData folder (%ProgramData%)

shell:Common Desktop   Public Desktop

shell:Common Documents   Public Documents

shell:Common Programs   All Users Programs, which are part of Start menu. Still used by the Start screen

shell:Common Start Menu   All Users Start Menu folder, same as above

shell:Common Startup   The Startup folder,
used for all users
shell:Common Templates   Same as above, but
used for new documents templates, e.g. by Microsoft
Office
shell:CommonDownloads   Public Downloads
shell:CommonMusic   Public Music
shell:CommonPictures   Public Pictures
shell:CommonRingtones   Public Ringtones
folder
shell:CommonVideo   Public Videos
shell:ConflictFolder   The Control Panel\All
Control Panel Items\Sync Center\Conflicts item
shell:ConnectionsFolder   The Control Panel\All
Control Panel Items\Network Connections item
shell:Contacts   Contacts folder (Address
book)
shell:ControlPanelFolder   Control Panel
shell:Cookies   The folder with IE's
cookies
shell:CredentialManager
C:\Users\<username>\AppData\Roaming\Microso
ft\Credentials
shell:CryptoKeys
C:\Users\<username>\AppData\Roaming\Microso
ft\Crypto
shell:CSCFolder   This folder is broken in
Windows 8/7, provides access to the Offline files item

shell:Desktop   Desktop

shell:Device Metadata Store

C:\ProgramData\Microsoft\Windows\DeviceMeta
dataStore

shell:DocumentsLibrary   Documents Library

shell:Downloads   Downloads folder

shell:DpapiKeys

C:\Users\<username>\AppData\Roaming\Microso
ft\Protect

shell:Favorites   Favorites

shell:Fonts   C:\Windows\Fonts

shell:Games   The Games Explorer item

shell:GameTasks

shell:HomeGroupFolder   The Home Group
root folder

shell:ImplicitAppShoC:\Users\<username>\AppDat
a\Local\Microsoft\Windows\GameExplorer

shell:History

C:\Users\<username>\AppData\Local\Microsoft\
Windows\History, IE's browsing history

shell:HomeGroupCurrentUserFolder   The Home
Group folder for the current user

rtcuts

C:\Users\<username>\AppData\Roaming\Microso
ft\Internet Explorer\Quick Launch\User
Pinned\ImplicitAppShortcuts

shell:InternetFolder   This shell command will
start Internet Explorer

shell:Libraries   Libraries

shell:Links   The "Favorites" folder from the Explorer navigation pane.

shell:Local AppData
C:\Users\<username>\AppData\Local

shell:LocalAppDataLow
C:\Users\<username>\AppData\LocalLow

shell:LocalizedResourcesDir This shell folder is broken in Windows 8

shell:MAPIFolder   Represents the Microsoft Outlook folder

shell:MusicLibrary   Music Library

shell:My Music   The "My Music" folder (not the Library)

shell:My Pictures   The "My Pictures" folder (not the Library)

shell:My Video   The "My Videos" folder (not the Library)

shell:MyComputerFolder Computer/Drives view

shell:NetHood
C:\Users\<username>\AppData\Roaming\Microsoft\Windows\Network Shortcuts

shell:NetworkPlacesFolder The Network Places folder which shows computers and devices on your network

shell:OEM Links   This shell command does nothing on my Windows 8 Retail edition. Maybe it works with OEM Windows 8 editions.

shell:Original Images   Not functional on Windows 8

shell:Personal   The "My Documents" folder (not the Library)

shell:PhotoAlbums   Saved slideshows, seems to have not been implemented yet

shell:PicturesLibrary   Pictures Library

shell:Playlists   Stores WMP Playlists.

shell:PrintersFolder   The classic "Printers" folder (not 'Devices and Printers')

shell:PrintHood
C:\Users\<username>\AppData\Roaming\Microsoft\Windows\Printer Shortcuts

shell:Profile   The User profile folder

shell:ProgramFiles   Program Files

shell:ProgramFilesCommon   C:\Program Files\Common Files

shell:ProgramFilesCommonX86   C:\Program Files (x86)\Common Files - for Windows x64

shell:ProgramFilesX86   C:\Program Files (x86) - for Windows x64

shell:Programs
C:\Users\<username>\AppData\Roaming\Microsoft\Windows\Start Menu\Programs (Per-user Start Menu Programs folder)

shell:Public   C:\Users\Public

shell:PublicAccountPictures
C:\Users\Public\AccountPictures

shell:PublicGameTasks
C:\ProgramData\Microsoft\Windows\GameExplor
er

shell:PublicLibraries
C:\Users\Public\Libraries

shell:Quick Launch
C:\Users\<username>\AppData\Roaming\Microso
ft\Internet Explorer\Quick Launch

shell:Recent   The "Recent Items" folder
(Recent Documents)

shell:RecordedTVLibrary   The "Recorded TV"
Library

shell:RecycleBinFolder   Recycle Bin

shell:ResourceDir   C:\Windows\Resources
where visual styles are stored

shell:Ringtones
C:\Users\<username>\AppData\Local\Microsoft\
Windows\Ringtones

shell:Roamed Tile Images   Is not implemented
yet. Reserved for future.

shell:Roaming Tiles
C:\Users\<username>\AppData\Local\Microsoft\
Windows\RoamingTiles

shell:SavedGames   Saved Games

shell:Screenshots   The folder for Win+Print Screen screenshots

shell:Searches   Saved Searches

shell:SearchHomeFolder   Windows Search UI

shell:SendTo   The folder with items that you can see in the "Send to" menu

shell:Start Menu

C:\Users\<username>\AppData\Roaming\Microsoft\Windows\Start Menu (Per-user Start Menu folder)

shell:Startup   Per-user Startup folder

shell:SyncCenterFolder   Control Panel\All Control Panel Items\Sync Center

shell:SyncResultsFolder   Control Panel\All Control Panel Items\Sync Center\Sync Results

shell:SyncSetupFolder   Control Panel\All Control Panel Items\Sync Center\Sync Setup

shell:System   C:\Windows\System32

shell:SystemCertificates

C:\Users\<username>\AppData\Roaming\Microsoft\SystemCertificates

shell:SystemX86

C:\Windows\SysWOW64 -Windows x64 only

shell:Templates

C:\Users\<username>\AppData\Roaming\Microsoft\Windows\Templates

shell:User Pinned   Pinned items for Taskbar
and Start screen,
C:\Users\<username>\AppData\Roaming\Microso
ft\Internet Explorer\Quick Launch\User Pinned
shell:UserProfiles   C:\Users, the users folder
where the user profiles are stored
shell:UserProgramFiles   Not implemented yet.
Reserved for future.
shell:UserProgramFilesCommon   same as above
shell:UsersFilesFolder   The current user profile
shell:UsersLibrariesFolder   Libraries
shell:VideosLibrary   Videos Library
shell:Windows   C:\Windows

shell:DpapiKeys
C:\Users\<username>\AppData\Roaming\Microso
ft\Protect
shell:Favorites   Favorites
shell:Fonts   C:\Windows\Fonts
shell:Games   The Games Explorer item
shell:GameTasks
C:\Users\<username>\AppData\Local\Microsoft\
Windows\GameExplorer
shell:History
C:\Users\<username>\AppData\Local\Microsoft\
Windows\History, IE's browsing history

shell:HomeGroupCurrentUserFolder   The Home
Group folder for the current user

shell:HomeGroupFolder   The Home Group
root folder

shell:ImplicitAppShortcuts
C:\Users\<username>\AppData\Roaming\Microso
ft\Internet Explorer\Quick Launch\User
Pinned\ImplicitAppShortcuts

shell:InternetFolder   This shell command will
start Internet Explorer

shell:Libraries   Libraries

shell:Links   The "Favorites" folder from
the Explorer navigation pane.

shell:Local AppData
C:\Users\<username>\AppData\Local

shell:LocalAppDataLow
C:\Users\<username>\AppData\LocalLow

shell:LocalizedResourcesDir   This shell folder is
broken in Windows 8

shell:MAPIFolder   Represents the Microsoft
Outlook folder

shell:MusicLibrary   Music Library

shell:My Music   The "My Music" folder
(not the Library)

shell:My Pictures   The "My Pictures" folder
(not the Library)

shell:My Video   The "My Videos" folder
(not the Library)

shell:MyComputerFolder   Computer/Drives view

shell:NetHood
C:\Users\<username>\AppData\Roaming\Microsoft\Windows\Network Shortcuts

shell:NetworkPlacesFolder   The Network Places folder which shows computers and devices on your network

shell:OEM Links   This shell command does nothing on my Windows 8 Retail edition. Maybe it works with OEM Windows 8 editions.

shell:Original Images   Not functional on Windows 8

shell:Personal   The "My Documents" folder (not the Library)

shell:PhotoAlbums   Saved slideshows, seems to have not been implemented yet

shell:PicturesLibrary   Pictures Library

shell:Playlists   Stores WMP Playlists.

shell:PrintersFolder   The classic "Printers" folder (not 'Devices and Printers')

shell:PrintHood
C:\Users\<username>\AppData\Roaming\Microsoft\Windows\Printer Shortcuts

shell:Profile   The User profile folder

shell:ProgramFiles   Program Files

shell:Programs
C:\Users\<username>\AppData\Roaming\Microso
ft\Windows\Start Menu\Programs (Per-user Start
Menu Programs folder)
shell:Public   C:\Users\Public
shell:PublicAccountPictures
C:\Users\Public\AccountPictures
shell:PublicGameTasks
C:\ProgramData\Microsoft\Windows\GameExplor
er
shell:PublicLibraries
C:\Users\Public\Libraries
shell:Quick Launch
C:\Users\<username>\AppData\Roaming\Microso
ft\Internet Explorer\Quick Launch
shell:Recent   The "Recent Items" folder
(Recent Documents)
shell:RecordedTVLibrary   The "Recorded TV"
Library
shell:RecycleBinFolder   Recycle Bin
shell:ResourceDir   C:\Windows\Resources
where visual styles are stored
shell:Ringtones
C:\Users\<username>\AppData\Local\Microsoft\
Windows\Ringtones
shell:Roamed Tile Images   Is not implemented
yet. Reserved for future.

shell:Roaming Tiles
C:\Users\<username>\AppData\Local\Microsoft\Windows\RoamingTiles

shell:SavedGames   Saved Games

shell:Screenshots   The folder for Win+Print Screen screenshots

shell:Searches   Saved Searches

shell:SearchHomeFolder   Windows Search UI

shell:SendTo   The folder with items that you can see in the "Send to" menu

shell:Start Menu
C:\Users\<username>\AppData\Roaming\Microsoft\Windows\Start Menu (Per-user Start Menu folder)

shell:Startup   Per-user Startup folder

shell:SyncCenterFolder   Control Panel\All Control Panel Items\Sync Center

shell:SyncResultsFolder   Control Panel\All Control Panel Items\Sync Center\Sync Results

shell:SyncSetupFolder   Control Panel\All Control Panel Items\Sync Center\Sync Setup

shell:System   C:\Windows\System32

shell:SystemCertificates
C:\Users\<username>\AppData\Roaming\Microsoft\SystemCertificates

shell:SystemX86
C:\Windows\SysWOW64 -Windows x64 only

shell:Templates
C:\Users\<username>\AppData\Roaming\Microsoft\Windows\Templates

shell:User Pinned   Pinned items for Taskbar and Start screen,
C:\Users\<username>\AppData\Roaming\Microsoft\Internet Explorer\Quick Launch\User Pinned

shell:UserProfiles   C:\Users, the users folder where the user profiles are stored

shell:UserProgramFiles   Not implemented yet. Reserved for future.

shell:UserProgramFilesCommon   same as above

shell:UsersFilesFolder   The current user profile

shell:UsersLibrariesFolder   Libraries

shell:VideosLibrary   Videos Library

shell:Windows   C:\Windows

USING THE <u>PING</u> UTILITY IN WINDOWS. ___

```
C:\Users\osorio>ping 127.0.0.1

Pinging 127.0.0.1 with 32 bytes of data:
Reply from 127.0.0.1: bytes=32 time<1ms TTL=64
Reply from 127.0.0.1: bytes=32 time<1ms TTL=64
Reply from 127.0.0.1: bytes=32 time<1ms TTL=64
Reply from 127.0.0.1: bytes=32 time<1ms TTL=64

Ping statistics for 127.0.0.1:
    Packets: Sent = 4, Received = 4, Lost = 0 (0% loss),
Approximate round trip times in milli-seconds:
    Minimum = 0ms, Maximum = 0ms, Average = 0ms

C:\Users\osorio>
```

Using the TraceROUTE Utility.

```
■ Command Prompt

C:\Users\osorio>tracert asu.edu

Tracing route to asu.edu [104.16.50.14]
over a maximum of 30 hops:

  1     5 ms     5 ms     1 ms  192.168.0.1
  2    25 ms    97 ms    34 ms  phnx-dsl-gw67.phnx.qwest.net [67.40.227.67]
  3    95 ms    41 ms    27 ms  phnx-agw1.inet.qwest.net [75.160.238.17]
  4    80 ms    84 ms   189 ms  los-brdr-02.inet.qwest.net [67.14.102.226]
  5    34 ms    34 ms    34 ms  63.146.27.250
  6   174 ms    37 ms    34 ms  cloudflare-ic-301668-las-bb1.c.telia.net [62.115.32.214]
  7    39 ms    52 ms   104 ms  104.16.50.14

Trace complete.

C:\Users\osorio>_
```

The command line CMD Help files.___

Just type at the C:/ **Help CMD** and then **<enter>** to access all of the CMD Help Files and commands.

```
C:\Users\osorio>help cmd
Starts a new instance of the Windows command interpreter

CMD [/A | /U] [/Q] [/D] [/E:ON | /E:OFF] [/F:ON | /F:OFF] [/V:ON | /V:OFF]
    [[/S] [/C | /K] string]

/C      Carries out the command specified by string and then terminates
/K      Carries out the command specified by string but remains
/S      Modifies the treatment of string after /C or /K (see below)
/Q      Turns echo off
/D      Disable execution of AutoRun commands from registry (see below)
/A      Causes the output of internal commands to a pipe or file to be ANSI
/U      Causes the output of internal commands to a pipe or file to be
        Unicode
/T:fg   Sets the foreground/background colors (see COLOR /? for more info)
/E:ON   Enable command extensions (see below)
/E:OFF  Disable command extensions (see below)
/F:ON   Enable file and directory name completion characters (see below)
/F:OFF  Disable file and directory name completion characters (see below)
```

```
Note that multiple commands separated by the command separator '&&'
are accepted for string if surrounded by quotes.  Also, for compatibility
reasons, /X is the same as /E:ON, /Y is the same as /E:OFF and /R is the
same as /C.  Any other switches are ignored.

If /C or /K is specified, then the remainder of the command line after
the switch is processed as a command line, where the following logic is
used to process quote (") characters:

    1.  If all of the following conditions are met, then quote characters
        on the command line are preserved:

        - no /S switch
        - exactly two quote characters
        - no special characters between the two quote characters,
          where special is one of: &<>()@^|
        - there are one or more whitespace characters between the
          two quote characters
        - the string between the two quote characters is the name
```

Laptop computers vs. Desktop computers vs. Notebook computers. ___Laptop computers were designed to be mobile, containing a battery that would provide from two to four hours of continuing use, and provide all the software and connections necessary to allow the user to work in a wireless environment. Laptops are now fabricated with great processor speeds and large amounts of memory and storage. Desktop computers are the more traditional form of computers built to be fixed in a home or office environment containing very large boxes with many drives and devices. These hardware boxes are generally heavy and are called " *chassis*" and they contain very large power supplies and storage drives that are heavy.

Notebook computers are usually very light and just have a basic operating system designed to provide the most minimum capabilities and connections. They are also limited in processor speed, memory and storage capability. Some notebook computers are now been built with similar capabilities like laptops, with very fast processors. The most popular laptops andnotebooks are made by HP (Hewlett Packard), Toshiba, Samsung, and others.

The Task Manager.__

Since computers are Task driven machines, and operate by tasks and processes, a Task Manager was built into the OS to manage and organize computer tasks for the user. Sometimes the user will overload the computer with multiple tasks at the same time, and the computer will freeze or crash as it runs out of memory trying to perform all of the tasks requested by the user. Sometimes the users will assume that computers are multitasking machines and they forget that to do multi-tasking, any computer must meet the following minimum criteria:

9. Must have large amounts of memory (8, 16, or 32 GB)

10. A very fast processor (Intel dual-core I-5 to I-7 or higher)
11. A large storage area (500 GB to 1.5 TB) Hard Drive

The Task Manager will also allow killing a process that hangs causing the computer to freeze, and also allowing the user that is logged on, to " disconnect himself" from the computer without login off.
You can access the Task Manager two ways: From the keyboard, press down at the same time, CTRL+ALT+DEL keys,
And also with the CTRL+SHIFT+ESC Keys.
The Task Manager will also show applications that are running, all of the Background processes as well as all of the Windows processes.
It will also show all of the applications that have an impact when your computer startup, and the services that are running in Windows.

The Antivirus Software Program on your Computer. All computers must have at least a basic Antivirus software program installed on the computer to provide protection against Viruses. Beware of Security programs that are available and claim to protect your computer from viruses, to protect your computer from viruses, you will need to have a full paid version or a basic Free version installed and configured on your computer. The Antivirus Software program should Scan your computer after it has been installed, your computer must be connected to the internet only to get the Virus Definition File Update. The Virus definition File updates your Antivirus program software, so that any known viruses or late published threats, will be known by your Antivirus program, before you run a Scan. Normally after the installation is done your Antivirus program will automatically connect via the internet and update its Definition file before running a Scan.

Once your Antivirus is updated, the next time you run a Scan on your computer; you must be disconnected from the Internet. to disconnect you may turn off your Router or Disable your Ethernet and or Wireless Network Adapters in the Control Panel. Once the scan is completed and no viruses are found, you can re-connect your computer to the Internet or turn back on your Router and or Network Adapter cards.

Run your Antivirus program at least once a week. And keep your Virus Definition File up to date.
Many Antivirus programs exist; the most popular paid versions are made by: Norton, MacAfee, Panda and others.
The Free basic Antivirus that is very popular is made by AVG.
AVG Antivirus can be downloaded from the Internet for free as well as others.

Both the Free versions and the paid versions will provide the protection you need. Do not connect your computer to the Internet if you do not have an Antivirus program installed on your machine. Beware of Trialware Antivirus programs that come with your computer, since they will expire in 30 to 60 days and do not offer any protection to your computer, since they are not a full version of the original software and do not contain all of the software modules. Most of them have no Virus Definition files to update.

When Antivirus Programs do not work. __ Most Antivirus programs will not work if their Virus Definition File (VDF) is not up to date.

CHAPTER EIGHT

VIRUSES THAT ATTACK WINDOWS COMPUTERS.____

Here is a list of the most common Viruses, and what they are:
VIRUS a program that spreads by replicating itself into other programs or documents.

WORM a self-replicating program, like a Virus, but does not attach itself. It's a self-contained program.

TROJAN a program that appears to be useful, but its not; and contains MALWARE , for example: A Utility

MALWARE Any software program designed to cause harm to your computer.

> HOAX VIRUS The worse kind of Virus, it sends hoax messages to users, from the infected computer.

ROOT KITS a very dangerous form of TROJAN, it monitors traffic to and from the infected computer, altering the system files and infecting other computers on the network, without the users knowing.

SPYWARE affects email, and monitors and control part of your computer, by decreasing the computer performance considerable, and infecting your email contacts.

SPAM a nuisance, not a program and not a threat, its unsolicited mail via email.

Protecting your Computer from Viruses. _____

You can protect your computer by installing a free or paid version of an Antivirus program. Many Antivirus programs are available from different manufacturers, they all protect your computer when properly installed, and with the Virus Definition file updated. A first time Scan is required before the program can begin to protect your computer. Before you start the next Scan, after you have done your first Scan, make sure that you are disconnected from the Internet, and or turn off momentarily your router. Then you may Scan your computer again.

The first time you Scan your computer you need to be connected to the Internet so that your Virus Definition file can get updated.

It is advisable to Scan your computer at least once a week.

A Security software program is not an Antivirus program and does not offer any protection against the many viruses that are a threat. Some Security software programs claim to protect your computer from viruses, only an Antivirus software program will protect your computer from viruses.

Your Computer Security. ___

Windows 7, 8 and 10 comes with some security
protection. They are two main security modules in
the Control Panel, one of them is called; Windows
Defender and the other is Windows Firewall. Make
sure that they are both turned on and are working.
Your Firewall must be always on to protect your
computer from threats.
Firewalls can be internal or external, and can be
software and or hardware. Having an external
Firewall box will greatly enhance the security
protection to your computer.

The Control Panel in Windows 7, 8 and 10 . __

The Control Panel is the heart of your computer. All
the modules running in the Control Panel are
performing a function so that your computer may
run smoothly.

To access the Control Panel, go to the Start or Run button in the lower left side of your Desktop, and select Settings, if the Control Panel is not visible in the menu, to bring up the Control Panel or if you are running Windows 8 you may also go to the Folder on the lower left side of your Desktop, and click on Computer, and the Control Panel will be displayed in the center Tabs that are visible. The Control Panel Icon Folder is unique and very different from any other folders.

A Control Panel Setting

Using the Maximum CPU Power in Windows 10.

Some applications in Windows are power-hungry applications,there is an option setting to max out the CPU, when more and faster power are needed to run the computer.
Right click the START menu and select Control Panel
Click Hardware and Sound
Select Power Option
Find Processor Power Management and open the menu for Minimum processor state.
Change the setting for **On Battery** to 100%
Change the setting for **Plugged in** to 100%
Click OK

Graphics Location

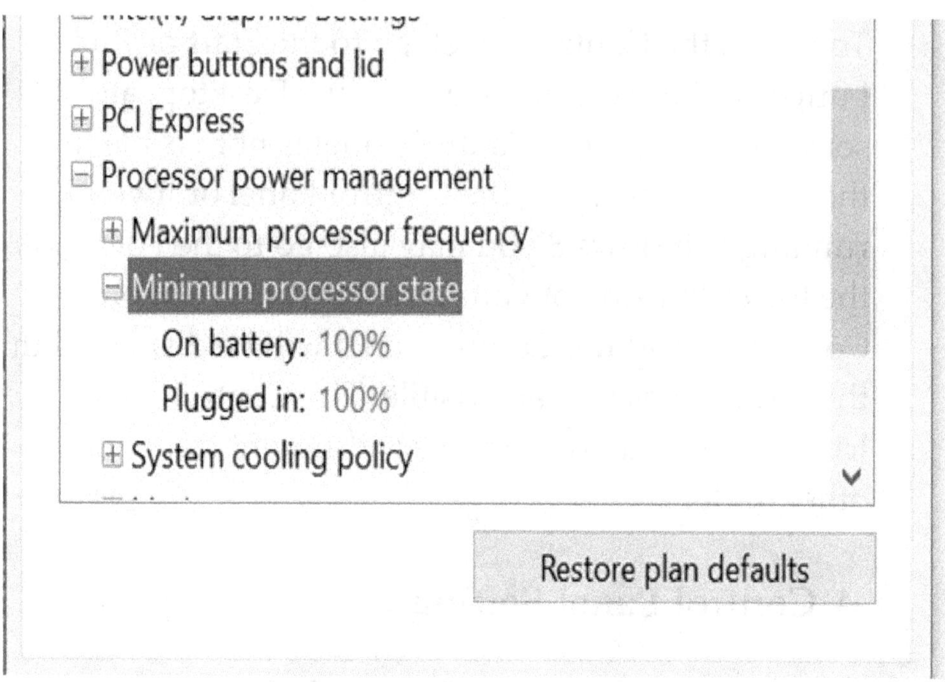

⊞ Power buttons and lid

⊞ PCI Express

⊟ Processor power management

　⊞ Maximum processor frequency

　⊟ Minimum processor state

　　On battery: 100%

　　Plugged in: 100%

⊞ System cooling policy

Restore plan defaults

Backup and Restore (Windows 7)

Find and fix problems

Network and Internet

View network status and tasks

Choose homegroup and sharing options

Hardware and Sound

View devices and printers

Add a device

Programs

Uninstall a program

Change default settings for media or devices   Play (

 Sound

Adjust system volume   Change system sounds   N

 Power Options

Region

Change power-saving settings   Change what the po

Change when the computer sleeps   Choose a powe

 Display

Make text and other items larger or smaller   How to

 Infrared

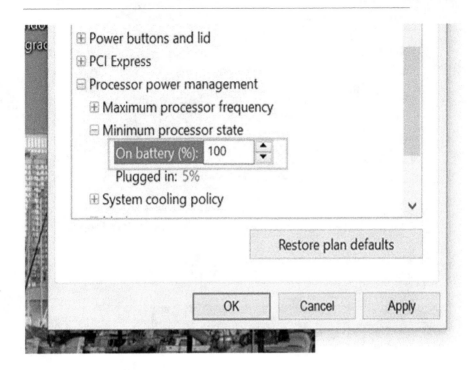

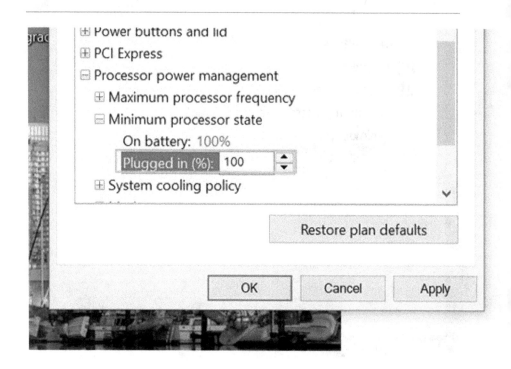

Done.

Administrative Users vs. Standard Users

In the Control Panel one of the most important controls is the User's Control Panel, where you can Create new Users for your computer and edit existing users. It is recommended that you first create a New User, when you get your computer for the first time. This New User would most likely be you. Once the user is created, you need to give the New User Administrative Rights, so that the user may have full control of the Computer. This user will then become the User Administrator. A Standard User will not have rights and privileges on the computer to do anything. As the Owner of your computer, you need to have full rights on your machine. Otherwise you will not be able to install or remove any software or do basic maintenance on your own machine, so this is a very first most important step, after getting your computer.

System Administrator vs. User Administrator

It is very important to know what is the System Administrator Password. If the Windows System Software gets corrupted, and needs to be re-installed; you will need to know the Administrator Password in order to get into the System to perform general maintenance and re installation of the system software. When Windows is installed for the first time on any machine, in the installation process, a password is requested for the *Administrator*, this password is important to know and remember, if you did not install your system and some one else did it; then you might be out of luck if you do not know the Administrator Password or Admin password. Most computers come with the Windows OS already installed, so the Admin password is not known. It is therefore important to get the original Windows Re-installation DVD, so that you may reinstall Windows if it gets corrupted or crashes.

Every new Computer should be provided with the Installation DVD included in the "sealed" Box and not in a Box with a Tape over it, which indicates that the Box was opened, and that the original DVD, Manuals and other User Documentation was taken out. Please note this as it is obvious that the Computer was not shipped to the store in a box with a Tape around it. All Computers are shipped in "sealed" boxes, there is no Tape involved.

The User Administrator only has rights and privileges over the user's machine and does not have any System administrator rights over any of the System software.
If the user tries to change, alter, modify etc.. Any system applications; a message will be displayed alerting the "User" that he or she does not have any rights or privilege to make or do the changes they want.
Please note that the User with Administrative privileges is not the same as the User Administrator.

CHAPTER NINE

COMPUTER NETWORKS, NETWORKING AND THE COMPUTER NETWORK CARDS OR ADAPTERS.

Let us define what Computer Networks are first, any computer that is connected to any other computer to share files and other applications is said to be connected to a Network. When computers need to share files and other software they are connected together in a LAN. A LAN is a Local Area Network. To facilitate this configuration, all computers have built in Network Cards.

They are two kinds of Network Cards also called NIC's, The first card or NIC is the " Ethernet Card" This is a special card that meets the International Standard for Networking called Ethernet (IEE 802.3) or Project 802, which is an IEEE Standard, accepted worldwide. The speed of this network card is 100 Mbps or 1 Gbps.,(Gigabit Ethernet) or higher.

The Gigabit Ethernet card is much fasterthan the 100 Mbps card and is desirable.

WIRELESS CARD OR ADAPTER. __

The second Network card is the Wireless card or WiFi card (802.11b/g/n) and the new standard ac/and /ad.
So the built in Wireless card should be (802.11 b/g/n or 802.11 b/g/n/ac or ad. This is the new Wireless Standard for the Network card that is preferred if you want to have a fast Network connection. If your Wireless card does not meet this standard, then it will be very slow and you will not be able to connect to the Internet. Your Wireless built in card must be at least (802.11 b/g/n) or higher.
Computers connect to the Internet through these cards. The connection to and from these cards is called Networking.

The settings for your Wireless and Ethernet cards are in the Control Panel,and it's called: "Networking and Sharing Center".

Networking is divided into LAN (Local Area Networks) and WAN (Wide Area Networks); The largest WAN in the world is the Internet.

Wireless adapters or cards are also installed into Printers which makes them " Wireless Printers" Most printers are now Wireless and require no cables, most printers are supplied with a USB (Universal Serial Bus) Cable, which is another Standard used in computers and networking.

WAN Networking requires special equipment and meets different standards with different kinds of cables and interfaces.

THE NETWORKING MODEL.___Networking is based on a Model accepted worldwide; it's called the OSI Networking Model or Open Systems Interconnect. Computer Network cards and Networking in general must follow this Model. All network cards are assigned a network protocol number or network ID that identifies the card on the Network. It is a special hexadecimal number (numbers and letters combined), this is also called in networking an IP (Internet Protocol) Address. This IP identifies the computer on a Network and is part of the Internet Protocol (TCP/IP) a Networking Standard. Without a TCP/IP address number the computer can not connect to the Internet or Network.

The speed of the computer Internet connection will depend on the built in Network cards. To find out what kind of Network cards is installed in your computer; go to the Control Panel to Network and Sharing Center and select "change adapter settings" to display the type and kind of network cards installed in the computer.

Networks and the Internet. ____

Networks are used to join computers and devices together and to share resources. The type of resources that are shared are: Information, Hardware, Software, and Data.

A Hardware resource that is shared could be a single connected Printer, that is shared via the Network to multiple Computers. These are shared through a LAN (Local Area Network) or a WAN (Wide Area Network.)To access the Internet services the user can connect via an ISP (Internet Service Provider) or via an OSP (Online Service Provider).

The main Internet Service is the World Wide Web (www.) and the Internet is the largest Network in the World.
The Internet is a worldwide collection of Networks that links individuals with resources and Data. The Internet have Millions of users and is growing more and more every day. The Web contains Billions of Documents called Web Pages.

The Internet Web Page Link. ___

A Web Page on the Internet may link to
other Web Documents, and to Text,
Graphics, Sound and Video.
A Web site (Google) may contain a
collection of related Web Pages. Computers
store Web Pages and the user, can use a
Web Browser such as IE (Internet Explorer
) or Firefox to view them.

The content of those Web Pages can be:
Financial Data, News, Guides, Weather,
Legal Information, other..
A very important Web document or link is:
" The Future of Internet 2) a New
Technology and Standard for the Internet
under Development by the World Wide
Web Consortium (wwwc.) or W3C.

CHAPTER TEN

THE INTERNET AND THE WORLD WIDE WEB (WWW).__

The Internet is the largest WAN (Wide Area Network) in the world. The internet is managed by the Internet Consortium **(ICANN)** Internet Consortium for Assigned Names and Numbers) and **ISO** International Standard Organization, which regulates standards and Protocols for the Internet as well as policies. The internet operates with Protocols and Standards that are accepted worldwide.

Computers and Windows consist of three modes for their proper operation;

Protocols, Standards and Policies.

Internet Protocols. ___

Protocols are a set of Rules that tell the computer hardware and software how to behave and operate. The Internet uses Protocols to make connections on the Internet and networks, and to regulate the World Wide Web (WWW.)

The Internet Protocols are: http and https (hypertext transport protocol), and www. Or World Wide Web protocol, these protocols must be typed into another protocol called the URL or Universal Resource Locator.

The protocol is then displayed as:

http://www. Google.com

As an example.

The Internet Domain. ____

The Internet Domain is considered a major part of the Internet Network. The Internet Network is comprised of the Internet WAN and LAN. The WAN is the Wide Area Network and the LAN is the Local Area Network. Both networks use different types of equipment and Protocols.

The Internet Domain is managed by ICANN (Internet Corporation for Assigned Names and Numbers.) this is one of the organizations that Regulates the Internet, and assigns all of the top level domains that are used on the Internet.

The Domain Names or name, is stored in a Server called DNS or Domain Name Server. This type of High Level Computer is used to translate Domain Names into IP Addresses.
For example; an IP Address that is: 198.80.146.30 once translated by the DNS, becomes the Domain Name:
www.scsite.com

The Web address and Web Page of an Internet site would be written as:
http://www.nmsu.edu/careers/index.html
Where, http:// is the Protocol, the Domain name is, **www.nmsu.edu** the Path is careers and index.html is the Web Page Name.

The Internet was developed in 1960 and the World Wide Web (www.) in 1990.

The Internet is identified as: " A World Wide Collection of Electronic Documents called a Web Page.
A " Web Browser" is the Application Software to access " Web Pages".

The Top Level Domains used on the Internet are:
.COM, .EDU, .BIZ, .INFO, .GOV, .MIL, .NAME, .PRO, .NET, .ORG, .AERO, and .COOP

CHAPTER ELEVEN

Using the Internet. _____
To use the Internet, computers require a Web Application called a "Browser" such as IE Internet Explorer, or Firefox. They are several Browsers available for use on the Internet. The most popular ones are, Internet Explorer, Firefox, Opera, Safari, etc.. A **Web Page** is created for each Web Application, for example; you can use Firefox as your Web Browser with Google as your Web Page.

The Internet begins by starting a service called " Internet Service," when Windows 7 or 8 start up., then running the Application software or Browser, to allow the user to view Web Sites on the World Wide Web and their respective Web Pages. A very popular Web Browser is IE or Internet Explorer developed by Microsoft., other popular Web Browsers are Firefox, developed by Mozilla and Safari developed by Apple Computers. Other Web Browsers are available on the Internet, and can be downloaded for free.

Each Web Page address will be displayed in the Web address URL (Universal Resource Locator) window.
In this window is where the Protocol HTTP: or HTTPS: should be typed,followed by the symbol // and the words: WWW. (World Wide Web) followed by the Internet address; for example:
http://www.nmsu.edu/index.html

The http is the Protocol, which stands for: Hypertext Transport Protocol, and www. Is also a Protocol that identifies the world wide web. The **www.nmsu.edu** is called the " Domain" and index.html displays the Web Page Name. All Web Pages are displayed by their Index, and html (Hypertext Markup Language) is the Computer Language used to develop the index and Web Pages.

Some Web Pages are also developed using another language called XML (Extensible Markup Language).

Free Web Browser Plug-Ins._____ To extend the capability of your Web Browser, you may install one or more " Plug-Ins " that will enhance the display of Multimedia Elements on the Web Page you are viewing. Some of the Free Plug-Ins available on the Internet for downloading are the following: Acrobat Reader, to view .pdf files on the Internet, or secure documents created with Acrobat in .pdf file format. FlashPlayer, from Macromedia.com, to view Graphic Animation on the Internet. , LiquidPlayer from liquidaudio.com to play Audio CD and MP3 audio files, RealOnePlayer, from Real.com to play and view live audio and video on the internet., Quicktime, from Apple.com to play HD Music audio and video on the Internet.; ShockwavePlayer, from Macromedia.com to play and view Multimedia 3D Graphics with HD audio and video, supporting Dolby 6.1 or higher and Surround Sound Formats.

Important Search Engines. ___

The software program contained in most Web Pages all have built in " Search Engines". The search engines are necessary for the user to be able to find what he or she is looking for. Some search engines will use the IP address or Internet Protocol Address, to search Web Sites and or Web Pages to find the information requested. Some Web Pages may contain one or more Search Engines.

The following are very important search engines on the Internet: HotBot.com, Excite.com, AlltheWeb.com, Altavista.com, AskJeeves.com, Lycos.com, LookSmart.com, Webcrawler.com, Overture.com, Infospace.com, etc...

Graphic Formats used on the Internet. ____

The following Graphic Formats are used on the **WWW**. And are: **.png** (Portable Network Graphics); **.gif** (Graphic Interchange Format); **.bmp** (Bitmap); **.pcx** (PC Paintbrush); **.jpeg** (Joint Photographic Experts Group);

.tiff (Tagged Image File Format).

Internet Protocol Address (IP.) uses the form: 198.80.146.30 or for example: 207.46.197.113 Which is equal to Microsoft Address: **www.microsoft.com** 207.46.197 identifies the Internet Network, and 113 identifies the Computer.

INTERNET WEB ADDRESSES vs. EMAIL ADDRESSES. __

Web addresses are different from Email addresses as they must contain the full Web Protocol, and is displayed as: **http://www.nmsu.edu** Email addresses are different as they only display the user name and At sign or @ with the ISP (Internet Service Provider) and is displayed as: johndoe@ yahoo.com or **marydoe@hotmail.com**

Standards.__

Standards are required on the Internet and all Computer Hardware and Software. The responsibility on these standards falls on an organization called ISO or International Standards Organization. This organization makes, changes, creates and modifies all standards for hardware and software. Standards are then divided into Proprietary, Defacto, National and International Standards, etc.. Some standards are open and accepted worldwide and becomes " defacto standards", such as HP standards for their Printers and other devices, and are HPGL (Hewlett Packard Graphic Language), PDL, Postscript Description Language, PDF Postscript Description File, etc..

Policies.___

Policies govern both hardware and software. Computer policies let the user's change the way computers behave and allow the users to modify the computer hardware to provide security on their system. An example is the Group Policy Editor or (GPEDIT.msc) a Microsoft Policy Editor and (SECPOL. msc) a Security Policy to set up your computer.

MMC Built In Utility. _____

The Microsoft Management Console or MMC is built into every computer running Windows, and provides policies and rules and regulations that are user friendly and allows the users to modify and change how some parts of their computers should operate, by turning on and or shutting down services that are not needed or required in Windows OS. To see the available policies and other software, type into the search area by the start button, the command: MMC to bring up the Microsoft Management Console. The MMC allows the user to create SNAPINS, small utility programs that allow the user to manage, clean and secure his computer. Many SNAPINS are already included in the MMC to use right away.

After typing MMC into the Start or Run window on the lower left side of the computer desktop, the MMC Console window will be displayed, just select " add or remove snapins" to view and or select the snapin you want to work with, or use the following step by step procedure:

The Microsoft Management Console (MMC) let users create much more flexible user interfaces and customize administration tools.

MMC unifies and simplifies day-to-day system management tasks. It hosts tools and displays them as consoles. These tools, consisting of one or more applications, are built with modules called snap-ins. The snap-ins also can include additional extension snap-ins. MMC is a core part of Microsoft's management strategy and is included in Microsoft Windows® operating systems. In addition, Microsoft development groups will use MMC for future management applications.

Microsoft Management Console enables system administrators and users to create special tools to delegate specific administrative tasks to users or groups. Microsoft provides standard tools with the operating system that perform everyday administrative tasks that users need to accomplish.

These are part of the **All Users** profile of the computer and located in the **Administrative Tools** group on the **Startup** menu. Saved as MMC console (.msc) files, these custom tools can be sent by e-mail, shared in a network folder, or posted on the Web. They can also be assigned to users, groups, or computers with system policy settings. A tool can be scaled up and down, integrated seamlessly into the operating system, repackaged, and customised.

Using MMC, system administrators can create unique consoles for workers who report to them or for workgroup managers. They can assign a tool with a system policy, deliver the file by e-mail, or post the file to a shared location on the network. When a workgroup manager opens the .msc file, access will be restricted to those tools provided by the system administrator.

Building your own tools with the standard user interface in MMC is a straightforward process. Start with an existing console and modify or add components to fulfill your needs. Or create an entirely new console. The following example shows how to create a new console and arrange its administrative components into separate windows.

Prerequisites and Requirements

There are no prerequisites: you don't need to complete any other step-by-step guide before starting this guide. You need one computer running either Windows 2000, Windows XP, Windows 7 , Windows 8 or Windows 10. For the most current information about hardware requirements and compatibility for servers, clients, and peripherals, see the Check Hardware and Software Compatibility page on the Windows website.

CHAPTER TWELVE

Creating Consoles with MMC

The most common way for administrators to use MMC is to simply start a predefined console file from the Start menu. However, to get an idea of the flexibility of MMC, it is useful to create a console file from scratch. It is also useful to create a console file from scratch when using the new task delegation features in this version of MMC.

Creating a New Console File (SNAP-IN)

c) On the Start Menu, click **Run**, type **MMC**, and then click **OK**. Microsoft Management Console opens with an empty console (or administrative tool) as shown in Figure 1 below. The empty console has no management functionality until you add some snap-ins. The MMC menu commands on the menu bar at the top of the Microsoft Management Console window apply to the entire console.

Figure 1: Beginning Console Window

Click Console (under Console1). On the Console Menu, click **Add/Remove Snap-in.** The Add/Remove Snap-in dialog box opens. This lets you enable extensions and configure which snap-ins are in the console file. You can specify where the snap-ins should be inserted in the **Snap-in's** "added to** drop-down box." Accept the default, **Console Root,** for this exercise.

d)Click **Add.** This displays the Add Standalone Snap-in dialog box that lists the snap-ins that are installed on your computer.

e) From the list of snap-ins, double-click **Computer Management** to open the **Computer Management** wizard.
   Click **Local computer** and select the check box for "**Allow the selected computer to be**

f) **changed when launching from the command line**."

g) Click **Finish**. This returns you to the **Add/Remove Snap-ins** dialog box. Click **Close**.

h) Click the **Extensions** tab as shown in Figure 2 below. By selecting the check box **Add all extensions**, all locally-installed extensions on the computer are used. If this check box is not selected, then any extension snap-in that is selected is explicitly loaded when the console file is opened on a different computer.

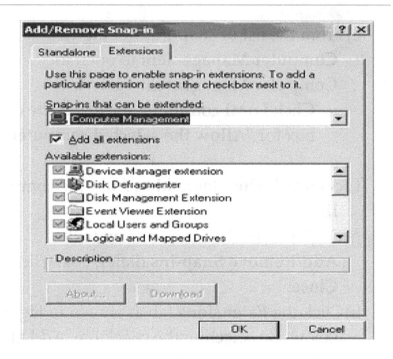

Figure 2: Select All Extensions

i) Click **OK** to close the Add/Remove Snap-in dialog box. The Console Root window now has a snap-in, **Computer Management**, rooted at the Console Root folder.

Customizing the Display of <u>Snap-ins in the Console</u>: New Windows

After you add the snap-ins, you can add windows to provide different administrative views in the console.

To add windows

1. **In the left pane of the tree view in Figure 3 below, click the + next to Computer Management. Click System Tools.**

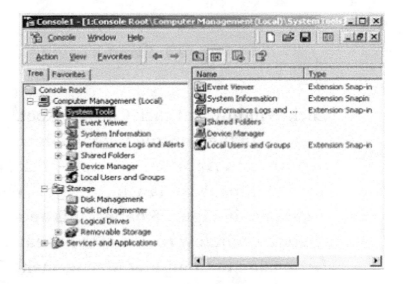

Figure 3: Console1: System Tools

2. Right-click the **Event Viewer** folder that opens, and then click **New window** from here. As shown in Figure 4 below, this opens a new Event Viewer window rooted at the Event Viewer extension to computer management.

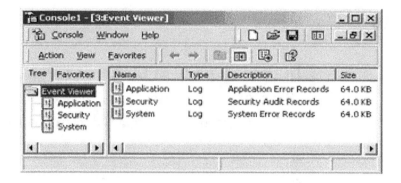

Figure 4: Event Viewer

3. Click **Window** and click **Console Root**.

    4.   **In the Console Root window, click Services and Applications, right-click Services in the left pane, and then click New Window. As shown in Figure 5 below, this opens a new Services window rooted at the Event Viewer extension to Computer Management. In the new window, click the Show/Hide Console Tree toolbar button to hide the console tree, as shown in the red circle in Figure 5 below.**

5. Close the original window with Console Root showing in it.

6. On the Window menu, select **Tile Horizontally**. The console file should appear and include the information shown in Figure 4 and Figure 5 above.

7. You can now save your new MMC console. Click the **Save as** icon on the Console window, and give your console a name. Your console is now saved as a .msc file, and you can provide it to anyone who needs to configure a computer with these tools.

8. **Note:** Each of the two smaller windows has a toolbar with buttons and drop-down menus. The toolbar buttons and drop-down menus on these each of these two windows apply only to the contents of the window. You can see that a window's toolbar buttons and menus change depending on the snap-in selected in the left pane of the window. If you select the View menu, you can see a list of available toolbars.

9. **Tip:** The windows fit better if your monitor display is set to a higher resolution and small font.

Creating Console Taskpads

If you are creating a console file for another user, it's useful to provide a very simplified view with only a few tasks available. Console taskpads help you to do this.

To create a console taskpad

From the Window menu, select New Window. Close the other two windows (you will save a new console file at the end of this procedure). Maximize the remaining window.

In the left pane, click the + next to the **Computer Management** folder, then click the + next to the **System Tools** folder. Click **System**, click the **Event Viewer** folder, right-click **System**, and select **New Taskpad** View.

Go through the wizard accepting all the default settings. Verify the checkbox on the last page is checked so that the Task Creation wizard can start automatically.

Choose the defaults in the Task Creation wizard until you come to the page shown below in Figure 6, then choose a list view task and select **Properties**:

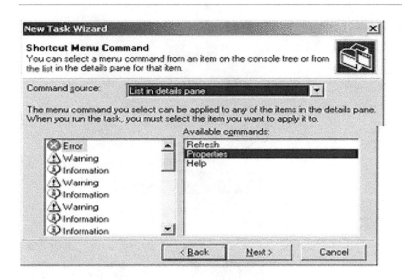

Figure 6: New Task Wizard

Click **Next** and accept the defaults for the rest of the screens. By selecting an Event and clicking **Properties**, you can see the property page for that Event.

After you click **Finish** on the last screen, your console should look like Figure 7 below:

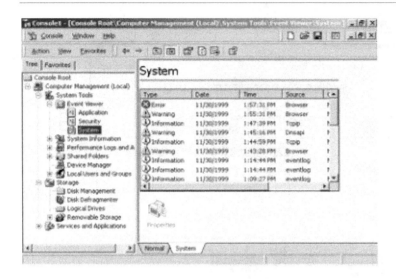

Figure 7: New Console Showing System Event Log

Click the **Show/Hide console tree** toolbar button.
From the view menu, click **Customize** and click each
of the options except the Description bar to hide each
type of toolbar.

The next section discusses how to lock the console
file down so that the user sees only a limited view.
For right now your console file should look like
Figure 8 below.

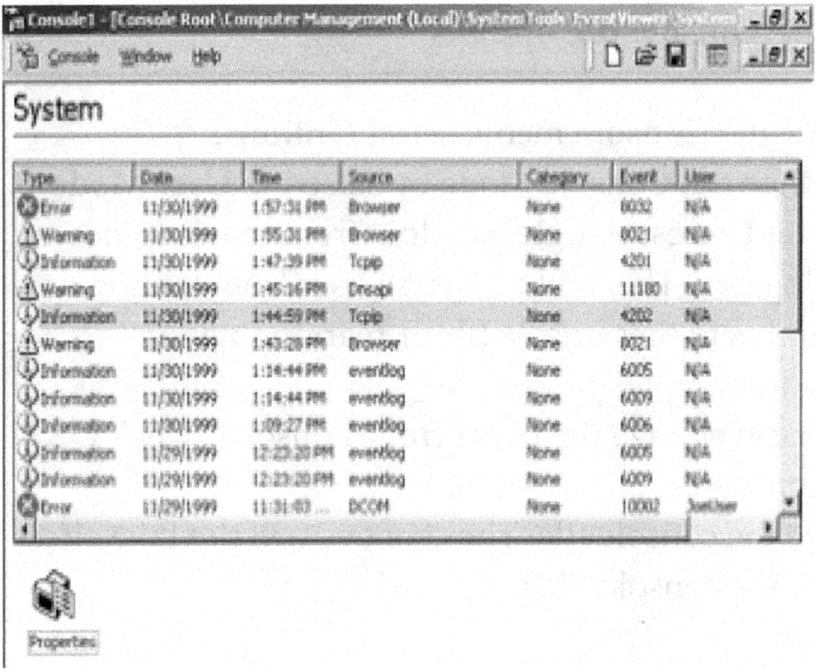

Figure 8: Customized View

Setting Console File Options

If you are creating a console file for another user, it is useful to prevent that user from further customizing the console file. The Options dialog box allows you to do this.

To set console file options

From the **Console** menu, select **Options**.
Change the Console Mode by selecting **User Mode limited access, single window** from the drop-down dialog box. This will prevent a user from adding new snap-ins to the console file or rearranging the windows.
You can change the name from Console1. Click **OK** to continue.
Save the console file. The changes will not take effect until the console file is opened again.

This is just one example of how the Microsoft Management Console lets you group information and functionality that previously would have required opening a Control Panel option plus two separate administrative tools. The modular architecture of MMC makes it easy for users to create snap-in Applications that leverage the platform while easing administrative load.

Built In MMC Snap-Ins. __

Microsoft has based most of its management applications on the Microsoft Management Console (MMC). The MMC provides a framework for building management consoles. Microsoft and many third-party application vendors have used this framework for creating their management consoles.

The MMC uses snap-ins for system and application management. Windows 7 & 8 comes with many built-in MMC snap-ins you can use to manage the system. You can use them to manage user settings, Windows applications, security, and many other vital aspects of the system.

Windows 7 & 8, and 10 contains the following built-in **MMC** snap-ins:

ActiveX Control – You can add individual ActiveX controls to view and configure. These Internet Explorer plug-ins add functionality to the browser.

Authorization Manager – You can set permissions for Authorization Manager-enabled applications.

Certificates – You can configure different certificate stores available on the system. Certificates help provide a secure operating environment. You can use them for identification, securing data and securing communications. There are certificate stores for users, applications, and the system itself.

Component Services – You can manage the system's COM+, or Component Services configuration. You can also configure Distributed Computer Object Model (DCOM) and Distributed Transaction Coordinator (DTC) settings. These are especially important when programs need to communicate between multiple computers.

Computer Management – This is actually a collection of snap-ins used for task scheduling, disk management, performance monitoring, and many other configuration and management tasks.

Device Manager – This is for viewing and configuring hardware installed on the system. You can disable devices, update drivers and troubleshoot potential issues.

Disk Management – This is for disk and volume management. You can create volumes, format disks and enable fault tolerance.

Event Viewer – This is for viewing system event logs that help you determine if your system or applications are having problems. You can also use the Security log to determine if there has been unauthorized access.

Folder – This is to add a folder for organizing your snap-ins, which comes in handy if you've added numerous snap-ins to a single MMC console.

Group Policy Object Editor – This lets you configure the Group Policy Objects on the system.

IP Security Monitor – This helps you monitor the status of your IP Security (IPsec) configuration, which secures communication between computers.

IP Security Policy Management – This helps you understand and configure the settings in your IPsec policy.

Link to Web Address – This lets you add a Web page to the MMC, which can be useful for applications and systems with Web-based management.

Local Users and Groups – This lets you configure users and groups on the local system, add user accounts, delete user accounts and configure various user properties.

NAP Client Configuration – This lets you configure Network Access Protection (NAP) client configuration settings.

Performance Monitor – This lets you monitor your system performance, including memory, hard disks, processors and a number of other components.

Print Management – This helps you manage print servers and printers connected to the system.

Resultant Set of Policy – This shows you what settings will be applied by your Group Policy settings, without actually applying them to the system.

Security Configuration and Analysis – This analyzes your configuration and security templates.

Security Templates – This lets you edit the security templates you applied to your system.

Services – This lets you view and configure properties for services running on the system. You can disable, start, stop or restart services; configure authentication and fault tolerance.

Shared Folders – This lets you view properties and status information for file shares. You can see what folders are being shared and who's accessing them.

Task Scheduler – This lets you schedule tasks to be automatically run at specified times or at specified intervals.

TPM Management – This lets you configure the Trusted Platform Module, which generates keys for cryptographic operations.

Windows Firewall with Advanced Security – This lets you configure Windows Firewall settings to control what processes, applications, and systems can access your system or generate network traffic from your system.

WMI Control – This lets you configure and manage the Windows Management Instrumentation (WMI) service, for managing and monitoring Windows systems.

The Fixed and Wireless Printer. ___

Many different kind of printers are available, but they all have something in common., the Print Engine inside the hardware., also all printers must meet the same international standards established by ISO and also Defacto Standards.

One of the most popular printer and also developer of the Printer print Engine as well as many Defacto Standards is, HP or Hewlett Packard Company. The Standards developed by HP became very popular and was accepted as a "Defacto" standard, which means in simple terms a standard used and adopted, by everyone and available Free in some cases.

Printers developed by other companies local or international will use HP Print Engine as well as HP Defacto Standards. HP developed many years ago de following standards now adopted worldwide. HPGL Hewlett Packard Graphic Language, PDL Postscript Description Language, HPGPIB Hewlett Packard General Purpose Interface Bus, PDF Postscript Description File, etc.. These Standards are now used in every Printer.

In addition to the HP Print Engine, the other part of the Printer hardware that is very important is the Printer " Gamut".
The Printer Gamut is an Array of All possible Colors that can be printer and or Displayed. The printer Gamut determines the Printer Resolution and capability to display and Print Millions of Colors following the International Color Standards.

In the beginning we could only print and display limited colors, 4 to 8 colors only with the Standard; RGB Red, Green and Blue.

Later on, other color Standards were developed, such as: CMYK(0) or, Cyan, Magenta, Yellow and K which represents zero (0) or (1).

When the K bit or Pixel was turned on; the color was White, when it was off (0) the color was Black.

This Standard gave printers the capability to Print 64 Colors or more.

New Standards were developed, like CROMALIN from Dupont, and PANTONE Certified Colors, which allowed the display and printing of Thousands and Millions of colors and shades.

In the mean time, Computer Monitors were developed to use the same Standards to allow for the display of millions of colors to offer High Resolution for Graphics, Video and Multimedia displays.

These same standards are used on Television sets today to display HD High Definition Graphics, Sound and Video., and very High Definition Displays (1080P) measured in Pixels.

Printers must meet the Color Standards and should have a large GAMUT (64 Bit) or higher; to allow the Printer to Print High Resolution Text and Graphics in many colors.

The Printer Memory. _____

Most printers should have enough RAM Memory installed to store FONTS and other Graphic Software. Printers should have at least 4Gb of RAM Memory installed.

The Printer Ports. _____

Most Printers should have at least two (2) USB Ports. The Standard USB Port is USB 2.0, the New Standard for USB (Universal Serial Bus) is USB 3.0 which is much faster.
The USB Ports are used to connect the Printer to the Computer USB Port so that the User can Print to the Printer., it requires a USB Cable that is included in most printers.

The Wireless Printer and Standard.____

Most Printers today are built with Wireless capabilities, also called Wi-Fi. As with Computers, Wi-Fi is built into the computer hardware and contains an Adapter called a Wireless Network

Adapter or Card

This Wireless card is now built into every computer and Printer, to give the hardware wireless capabilities.

Wireless technology or Wi-Fi must meet the Wi-Fi Standard 802.11
That is defined as 802.11 a/b/g that originally only supported 54 Mbp and operated in 2.4 Mhz and 5.0 Mhz frequencies.

Later on a new standard 802.11 a/b/g/**n** was developed that increased the data rate to 100 Mbps and operated at higher frequencies.

The New Standard that was released last year is 802.11 a/b/g/n/**ac** and **ad**. This New Standard allows Wi-Fi to operate at very high Frequencies of 20 and 60 GHz. Increasing the data rate to Gigabit speeds and beyond.

Wi-Fi capable Printers are easy to use and setup, as no cables is required and the Printer is detected by the Network immediately as just another device. The built-in software will automatically setup the printer for the user.

At the publication of this book, information of the new Windows 11 is emerging. If there will be a new Windows 11, then we should expect great things from this technology, as we the users are driving the technology. We are demanding new and better software and faster processors, as we strive to make the Internet FREE for everyone.

We shall see what the future brings us, and hope the technology will benefit all users worldwide.

Basic Computer Terms

Bit - A binary unit of data storage that can only be a value of 0 or 1.

BIOS - BIOS stands for Basic Input/Output System and it is a low level program used by your system to interface to computer devices such as your video card, keyboard, mouse, hard drive, and other devices.

Boot - A term used to describe what happens to a computer when it is turned on, the operating system begins to run, and then the user is able to use the computer successfully.

Byte - 8 bits of data which has a possible value from 0 to 255.

CD-ROM disk - A disk with about 640Mb of storage capacity which are more commonly read than written to.

CD-ROM drive - The hardware component that is used to read a CD-ROM or write to it.

Crash - A common term used to describe what happens to a computer when software errors force it to quit operating and become unresponsive to a computer user.

Driver - A specially written program which understands the operation of the device it interfaces to, such as a printer, video card, sound card or CD ROM drive. It provides an interface for the operating system to use the device.

File - A collection of data into a permanent storage structure. Stored on a permanent storage media such as a computer hard drive.

Firmware - Software written into permanent storage into the computer.

Floppy disk - A low capacity storage media which can be written to as easily as it is read.

Floppy Drive - The hardware component that is used to read or write to a floppy disk.

Hardware - Describes the physical parts of your computer which you can physically touch or see such as your monitor, case, disk drives, microprocessor and other physical parts.

Internet - A network of networks which incorporate a many organizations, physical lines, the ability to route data, and many services including email and web browsing.

ISP - Internet Service Provider is an organization that provides the ability to connect to the internet for their customers. They also usually provide additional services such as e-mail and the ability to host web sites.

MIME - multipurpose internet mail extension

Memory - Used to provide the temporary storage of information function.

Network - A general term describing to the cables and electronic components that carry data between computers. It is also generally used to refer to the server computers that provide services such as printing, file sharing, e-mail, and other services.

Operating System - The core software component of a computer providing the ability to interface to peripheral and external devices along with program functions to support appllication programs.

Parallel - A data transmission method where data is sent on more than one line at a time. This may be any number of bits at a time, but is usually one word at a time (two bytes) or possibly three bytes at a time.

Protocols - A standard method used for communications or other internet and network functions.

Security flaw - A software bug allowing an attacker a method to gain unauthorized access to a system.

Serial - A data transmission method where data is sent on a single line and one bit is sent at at a time. This is similar to a line which one item must come one after another

Software - Describes the programs that run on your system.

SPAM - A term used to describe junk and unsolicited e-mail.

Storage Media - A term used to describe any magnetic device that computer data can be permanently stored on such as a hard drive or floppy drive.

URL - Uniform Resource Locator is the term used to describe a link which points to a location of a file on the internet.

Virus - A program that runs on a system against the owner's or user's wishes and knowledge and can spread by infecting files or sending itself through e-mail

Vulnerability - Software errors that allow some kind of unauthorized access when they are used or exploited.

Word - Two bytes or 16 bits of data with a possible unsigned value from 0 to 16535.

Worm - A term used to describe an unwanted program that uses system or application vulnerabilities to infect a computer without the user doing anything but connecting to an infected network.

Computer Abbreviations

Operating Systems and Data Storage

- BIOS - This is the Basic Input Output System which controls the computer, telling it what operations to perform. These instructions are on a chip that connects to the motherboard.

- BYTE - A byte is a storage unit for data.

- "K" is a Kilobyte which is 1024 bytes.

- "MB" is a Megabyte which is a million bytes.

- "GB" is a Gigabyte, which equals 1000 megabytes.

  - CPU - This stands for the Central Processing Unit of the computer. This is like the computer's brain.
  - MAC - This is an abbreviation for Macintosh, which is a type of personal computer made by the Apple Computer company.
  - OS - This is the Operating System of the computer. It is the main program that runs on a computer and begins automatically when the computer is turned on.
  - PC - This is the abbreviation for personal computer. It refers to computers that are IBM compatible.
  - PDF - This represents the Portable Document Format which displays files in a format that is ready for the web.

- RAM - This stands for Random Access Memory which is the space inside the computer that can be accessed at one time. If you increase the amount of RAM, then you will increase the computer's speed. This is because more of a particular program is able to be loaded at one time.
- ROM - This is Read Only Memory which is the instruction for the computer and can not be altered.
- VGA - The Video Graphics Array is a system for displaying graphics. It was developed by IBM.
- WYSIWYG - This initialism stands for What You See Is What You Get. It is pronounced "wizziwig" and basically means that the printer will print what you see on your monitor.

Connecting to the Internet

- FTP - This is a service called File Transport Protocol which moves a file between computers using the Internet.

- HTML - HyperText Markup Language formats information so it can be transported on the Internet.
- HTTP - Hypertext Transfer Protocol is a set of instructions for the software that controls the movement of files on the Internet.
- IP - This stands for Internet Protocol which is the set of rules that govern the systems connected to the Internet. IP Address is a digital code specific to each computer that is hooked up to the Internet.
- ISP - The Internet Service Provider is the company which provides Internet service so you can connect your computer to the Internet.
- LAN - This stands for Local Area Network which is the servers that your computer connects to in your geographic area.
- PPP - Point-to-Point Protocol is the set of rules that allow your computer to use the Internet protocols using a phone line and modem.
- URL - This is the Uniform Resource Locator which is a path to a certain file on the World Wide Web.

- USB - The Universal Serial Bus is used for communications between certain devices. It can connect keyboards, cameras, printers, mice, flash drives, and other devices. Its use has expanded from personal computers to PDAs, smartphones, and video games, and is used as a power cord to connect devices to a wall outlet to charge them.
- VR - Virtual Reality simulates a three-dimensional scene on the computer and has the capability of interaction. This is widely used in gaming.
- VRML - Virtual Reality Mark-up Language allows the display of 3D images.

Common Email Abbreviations

Here is a list of **email abbreviations** that are commonly used to get your point across in less time and fewer keystrokes:

- 2G4U - Too Good For You
- AWHFY - Are We Having Fun Yet?
- AYPI - And Your Point Is?
- GAL - Get A Life

- GMTA - Great Minds Think Alike
- J4F - Just For Fun
- KISS - Keep it Simple, Stupid
- QL - Quit Laughing!
- RUOK - Are you Okay?
- SITD - Still In The Dark
- TIC - Tongue In Cheek
- WYSIWYG - What You See Is What You Get
- YYSSW - Yeah Yeah Sure Sure Whatever
- ZZZ - Sleeping, Bored, Tired

- AWGTHTGTTA - Are We Going To Have To Go Through That Again?

New Technologies.

ABOUT THE NEW USB 3.1 and C-CONNECTOR STANDARD.

The last major update to the ever-evolving USB standard came in 2013 with USB 3.1, and that was accompanied by the introduction of the new USB-C connector. If anything, it could become the default connection standard for even more devices.

Apple helped kick off the trend with the 12-inch **MacBook** that used a single USB-C socket to not just connect to all its peripherals, but also to provide power.

USB-C – it is not a new standard

The first thing to realize about USB-C is that it's not a new USB standard in the same way as USB 1.1, USB 2.0, USB 3.0 or the very latest USB 3.1 are. Those upgrades focus on defining what the connection can do in terms of speed and feature improvements, whereas USB-C is all about the physical connection, like with microUSB and miniUSB.

USB 3.0

USB 3.0 was a big change as it brought new connector types to allow for its extra speed and power draw, with them often colored blue to denote their prowess. **USB 3.0 can run at up to 5Gbps, delivering 5V at 1.8A. It arrived in November 2008.**

USB 3.1

The latest and greatest version of USB was released in July 2013, though uptake is still almost non-existent. **It can deliver 10Gbps of throughput while up to 2A can be drawn over 5V, and optionally either 5A over 12V (60W) or 20V (100W). This is the reason the new MacBook can be powered just by its USB connection.**

USB 2.0

The second version of USB arrived in April 2000 and it provided a massive boost **in maximum data throughput, up to 480Mbps. Power draw was also increased to a maximum of 1.8A at 2.5V.**

USB-C

This brings us to USB-C. Where Type-A and Type-B have had to work within the framework of being backwards compatible, Type-C is intended to replace both and is designed to be small enough to not need any mini or micro variants. The intention is that it will completely replace all types of USB on both host and client devices.

What's more **its headline feature is of course that it's reversible. This means you no longer have to get the plug the right way round – or even the cable the right way round** – but instead, like Apple's Lightning connection, it'll work whichever direction you try – no more USB superposition.

To enable this USB-C cables actually require circuitry to tell which way round they are and route power and data in the right way, just like on Apple's Lightning connection. This is unlike all existing USB standards which are just 'dumb' cables.

USB-C also builds on the new USB 3.1 standard so to all intents and purposes is the connection type that brings in the new power and speed advantages of USB 3.1.

USB-C is still backwards compatible with existing USB variants, but that of course requires adapters.

The company responsible for certifying the USB Type-C standard has announced steps to protect against dodgy cables.

USB Type-C has been taking off steadily over the past year or so, with the likes of the **MacBook** showcasing the connection standard's advantages.

The standard is compact, reversible, and capable of both fast charging and data transfer.

However, USB-C (as it's also known) has had a problem with dodgy cables that don't quite meet up to the full standards required. Indeed, some can actively damage the host device under certain circumstances.

Now the USB-IF has **announced** measures to solve this issues. **The USB Type-C Authentication specification is a protocol that enables devices to confirm the authenticity of USB devices or chargers at the point of connection, before any power or data can be transferred.**

This authentication data is transmitted using 128-bit encryption, so it's secure.

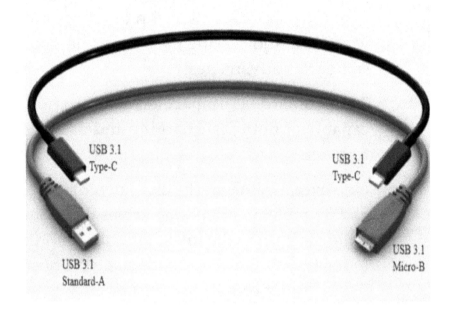

This is not the End.